The Educated Listener

A NEW APPROACH TO MUSIC APPRECIATION

By Jaren S. Hinckley

Brigham Young University

cognella®
academic publishing

Bassim Hamadeh, CEO and Publisher
Michael Simpson, Vice President of Acquisitions
Jamie Giganti, Managing Editor
Jess Busch, Graphic Design Supervisor
Becky Smith, Acquisitions Editor
Monika Dziamka, Project Editor
Stephanie Sandler, Licensing Associate
Mandy Licata, Interior Designer

First published in the United States of America in 2014 by Cognella, Inc.

Trademark Notice: Product or corporate names may be trademarks or registered trademarks, and are used only for identification and explanation without intent to infringe.

Cover image copyright © 2011 by Depositphotos Inc./Arkady Chubykin
Interior image copyright © 2013 Depositphotos/Lakalla

Printed in the United States of America

ISBN: 978-1-62131-747-0 (pbk)/ 978-1-62131-748-7 (br)

www.cognella.com   800-200-3908

Contents

CLASSICAL ERA (1750–1830)

ROMANTIC ERA (1810–1910)

TWENTIETH CENTURY (1900–2000)

CONTEMPORARY ERA (1960–PRESENT)

POPULAR MUSIC

This book would not have been possible without the help of my friend and former student, Abigail Tippetts. Her editing skills, musical knowledge, and sense of humor were invaluable.

Introduction

This textbook is designed to aid anyone—regardless of musical knowledge—in developing skills needed for creatively and intelligently discussing and listening to music. By learning about the musical genres, forms, and techniques used by composers of Western classical music, you will gain a greater understanding of and appreciation for the art of music. You will become an educated listener.

In order to increase your musical knowledge effectively and quickly, here are some suggestions:

USE THE TEXT WISELY: This text is a giant glossary. Entries include a basic definition followed by a more detailed explanation. If you encounter a word that you do not understand, it is likely explained somewhere else in the text. Referring to the index will lead you to the correct information.

ASK QUESTIONS: At times, you may not understand something you hear on the radio, something you read in CD liner notes, in a program, or something the conductor or performer says prior to a performance. If this happens, ASK! Ask a musically knowledgeable friend. Ask a music instructor. Refer to this book! Don't be discouraged if you have a steep learning curve when it comes to grasping these new concepts. Do not be embarrassed to ask questions; asking leads to learning.

LISTEN TO CLASSICAL MUSIC: Find out if you have a local classical radio station. If you're unsure, search online using the name of your city and "classical radio" as the keywords and see what comes up. Another option is listening on the Internet. Many classical radio stations have live streaming or an app that allows you to listen to that station online or on your smartphone. Once you have found a station or online source, you can immediately begin to increase your musical knowledge by paying attention to the things the announcer says about the music. Pandora.com, Rhapsody.com, Naxos.com, and iTunes are a few of the online programs, apps, and websites that can help you increase your listening opportunities. Some of these programs require a subscription fee, but others are free.

ATTEND MUSICAL EVENTS: Every large city and many small towns have professional or community orchestras, performing arts centers that host chamber music concerts and other artistic events. Most universities have student and faculty recitals throughout the year—and many are free of charge. Whatever the venue, attend them! When you attend events like these, get a program and read it. Programs list the pieces to be performed, and many programs also contain program notes explaining various details about each piece on the program. You will learn a lot about music and its terminology by doing this simple thing.

AVOID SNAP JUDGMENTS: A lot of people make statements like "I hate opera" because at one time they had an initial negative reaction to it. If you give different styles of classical music multiple chances, you will discover that you like certain performers and composers better than others, but you'll never know what you like until you start listening. For example, I used to dislike opera, but after listening to examples of opera through various classes and performances, I discovered that there were certain operas (and certain composers) that I truly enjoyed. I am now much more willing to explore different genres and I learn something each time I do. My life is much richer as a result of my exposure to music—all kinds of music.

SUGGESTIONS FOR INSTRUCTORS

The primary purpose of introductory music history classes is to help students develop a love and understanding of classical music. Every instructor has his/her own unique approach to teaching. This text:

- is designed to help instructors pick and choose concepts they feel are most important to teach.

- focuses on the genres and forms that students are most likely to encounter at concerts, on the radio, at church services, and throughout their lives.
- does not attempt to cover all facets of music history; it presents the main genres, forms, styles, techniques, and basic information about the best-known composers from each time period.

The composer lists found at the end of each section are to provide both instructor and student a myriad of study options.

TEXT LAYOUT: It is not necessary to proceed chapter by chapter. Maybe you will want to start with the Contemporary Era and work backwards; perhaps you prefer to skip the Middle Ages and the Renaissance; or you may want to organize your class by genre. This text is designed for flexibility so you can choose which topics to focus on and in what order you will proceed. If you prefer to teach a particular form in conjunction with a particular genre (found in a different chapter), by all means, do it! For example, I may want to teach ground bass in conjunction with the genre of opera. In that case, I would assign students to read about Baroque opera in one chapter and ground bass in another.

READING ASSIGNMENTS: Because this text is essentially a large glossary, you can teach using a variety of approaches. Some professors prefer to introduce students to concepts in class and then assign readings that follow up and reinforce the knowledge gained. Others prefer to have the students read in advance so class time can be spent listening to music and discussing concepts that have already been studied. Others do a mix of both. Be creative!

LISTENING EXAMPLES: Because of the diversity of resources available to students and the lack of flexibility involved with sticking to a specific set of CDs, I have chosen to not provide a CD set with this textbook. This gives you the flexibility and freedom to create your own listening playlists using whatever online resources you have at your disposal. Most university libraries have subscriptions to online listening libraries such as Naxos, Classical Music Library, or Music Online, to name a few. These online services allow faculty to create listening lists with more flexibility than ever before. This text offers *suggested* listening for each genre and composer, but individual instructors should still create personalized listening lists geared directly to the topics being taught.

LISTENING CHARTS: In addition, most textbooks have listening charts that the students can follow along with as they listen. Because this text relies on individual instructors' personalized playlists for the listening examples, there

XII | THE EDUCATED LISTENER: A NEW APPROACH TO MUSIC APPRECIATION

is no way to include second-by-second listening charts. This should not be a problem; students learn material and retain it more deeply by being provided with a general chart of a particular form (like ritornello, sonata, or fugue) to follow along with the assigned listening. You may want to consider having students listen together in a "study group" setting to ensure that, through their collective intelligence, they succeed. The professor can then follow up at the next class session to see how students fared. Alternatively, individual professors can provide his/her own listening charts with a play-by-play to help the students in their at-home listening.

ASSIGNMENTS: Numerous studies have shown that students learn through discussion, experience, and application. At the end of entries (found in each chapter) are "Further Investigation" assignments and "Suggested Listening." These are intended for use either in class to facilitate discussion, or as assignments for students to complete between class sessions or as a follow-up or prelude to class instruction.

As the author of this text, it is my hope that you will find this a fun and new way of teaching introductory music history. It provides freedom for you to teach the topics you want to teach using the listening examples you want to use.

The future patrons of classical music are in your hands—help them become educated listeners and music lovers!

PRELUDE

Components of Music

THE BASICS

Pitch

A **pitch** is a sound created by vibrations. More specifically, pitch refers to how high or low a particular sound is. If the vibration is fast, the pitch will be high; if it is slow, the pitch will be low. In string instruments, the sound is produced by the vibrating strings; in the human voice, by the vibrating vocal cords; and in brass and woodwind instruments, the vibrating reed, lips, or column of air.

Note

A **note** is a single pitch. Oftentimes, people use the words "pitch" and "note" interchangeably.

Chord

A **chord** is two or more notes played at the same time. There are certain kinds of chords that sound more "normal" to our Western ears, for instance the major triad. Sing "Do-Mi-Sol" to hear the three notes used in a major triad.

Consonance/Dissonance

Consonance is when music features notes that sound nice together—no real sense of discord or tension. Consonant moments sound conclusive or at rest.

Dissonance is when music features notes that don't sound nice together—there is a sense of discord or tension. Dissonant moments sound transitional or uneasy.

While these are certainly subjective judgments, when one note is sounded at the same time as another note, the listener has an immediate sense of dissonance or consonance.

Many composers choose to use dissonance sparingly, allowing brief moments of tension to develop before they "resolve" to a consonance. Other composers use dissonance non-stop because they want the listener to feel unsettled for the entire piece of music. Still others don't find dissonance to be that unsettling; they enjoy it.

Interval

An **interval** is the distance between any two pitches. These are the main intervals:

Minor second: A dissonant interval. To hear a minor second, play any key on the piano and then the very next key (regardless of color), or sing the first two notes of the *Jaws* theme. This is also known as a "half step."

Major second: A mildly dissonant interval. Sing the first two notes of a major scale ("Do – Re") and you'll hear a major second. This is also known as a "whole step."

Minor third: A slightly dissonant interval. Sing the first two notes of *Greensleeves* (also known as *What Child Is This?*).

Major third: A consonant interval. Sing "Do – Mi," or the first two notes of *I Heard the Bells on Christmas Day*.

Perfect fourth: A consonant interval. Sing "Do – Fa" or the first two notes of *Here Comes the Bride*.

Tri-tone (also known as an augmented fourth, a diminished fifth, or "the devil's interval"): A very dissonant interval. Sing the first two syllables of "Maria" from *West Side Story* or sing the words "The Simpsons," which is the very first thing you hear SUNG at the start of the theme song—the first two syllables ("The Simp-") make a tri-tone.

Perfect fifth: An extremely consonant interval. Sing "Do – Sol" or *Twinkle Twinkle Little Star*—when you move from the first twinkle to the second twinkle, you have sung a perfect fifth.

Minor sixth: A somewhat dissonant interval. Sing the first two notes of "Close Every Door" from *Joseph and the Amazing Technicolor Dreamcoat*. Or, sing the first four notes of Joplin's *The Entertainer*; the third and fourth notes are a minor sixth (and so are the fifth and sixth notes, and the seventh and eighth notes).

Major sixth: A consonant interval. Sing "Do – La" or the first two notes of *My Bonnie Lies Over the Ocean* or the NBC jingle.

Minor seventh: A dissonant interval. Sing the first two notes of "Somewhere" from *West Side Story*.

Major seventh: A very dissonant interval. Sing "Do – Ti" or the first two notes of the chorus of *Take On Me* by a-ha. Or, if you are familiar with 80's television theme songs, the first two notes of the theme song to *Fantasy Island*.

Octave: The most consonant interval. Sing "Do-Re-Mi-Fa-Sol-La-Ti-Do"—the first and last "Do" create an octave. Or you can sing the first two notes of the chorus of "Somewhere Over the Rainbow" from *The Wizard of Oz*.

Unison: A unison is the same note sung or played by more than one person. (It is technically not a true "interval" since there is no distance between the two notes.)

Scale

A **scale** is a succession of whole-step and half-step intervals that sound "normal" or logical to our Western ears.

There are three main types of scales used in Western music today—**major**, **minor**, and **chromatic**.

Major scale: A major scale is created by playing the succession of whole steps (W) and half steps (H) indicated on the illustration below. Sing "Do-Re-Mi-Fa-Sol-La-Ti-Do" and you will have sung a major scale.

W   W   H   W   W   W   H

Minor scale: A minor scale is created by playing a different succession of whole and half steps.

W   H   W   W   H   W   W

Chromatic scale: A chromatic scale is created by playing only half steps—no whole steps.

By following the above successions of intervals, anyone can play these scales starting on any note.

Melody

A **melody** is a succession of notes—any succession of notes. Composers choose which pitches and intervals they want to use in their melody. In very general terms, the melody is the "catchy, hummable" part of a piece of music.

Because melody is such a general term, there are other terms that are helpful in describing a particular piece of music.

Phrase: A **phrase** is a short melody, that, if you were singing, it would feel quite natural to take a breath at the end of it. For instance, "Jingle Bells, Jingle Bells, Jingle all the way (breath). Oh what fun it is to ride in a one-horse open sleigh (breath)." Or for a slower example, "Silent Night, (breath) Holy Night, (breath), all is calm, (breath), all is bright (breath)."

Motive: A **motive** is a short succession of notes that is used throughout a piece of music to create a sense of unity within the piece. Motives can be melodic or rhythmic. One of the most famous motives in music history is the first four notes of Beethoven's *Symphony No. 5* (dum-dum-dum-DUUUUUUM).

Theme: A **theme** is similar to a motive, but longer. The opening clarinet solo in Gershwin's *Rhapsody in Blue* is a good example. It is heard right at the beginning of the piece, played by the clarinet, then it comes back time and time again played by various instruments within the orchestra.

Harmony

Harmony is musical material that enhances or supports the melody. Any other notes that occur at the same time as a melody can be considered part of the harmony. For instance, in most hymns or music sung by choirs, it is customary to have four-part harmony—the melody line, the alto line, the tenor line, and the bass line. Aside from the melody line, the other three parts are considered harmony. (Harmony features notes lined up vertically on the page, while melody features notes lined up horizontally.)

STRUCTURAL ELEMENTS

Key/Tonality/Atonality

A **key** is an organizing principle within a composition. Key is determined by the first note in the scale; in other words, if a scale begins on the note called "C," and a piece is composed using the notes in the "C" scale, we would say that that piece is written in the "key of C."

Every note within a scale has a functional name as labeled here:

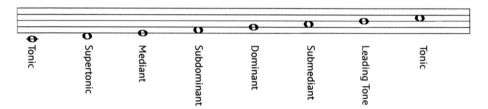

The first note of each scale is called the **tonic**. Turn on a piece of music and listen for a moment, then start to hum the note that seems to be the most prominent overall. You will likely find that you are humming the tonic. The tonic acts as a homing signal that draws us in throughout the music and provides a sense of conclusiveness at the end of a piece of music. The tonic is most obvious in the bass line. You may notice that occasionally, when you are humming the tonic, it goes away and you can't find it for a few moments and then it comes back. The bass line has most likely moved to the subdominant or dominant notes briefly before returning to the tonic. The word that describes what happens when a piece of music moves from one key to another is **modulation**. The composer "modulates" the piece from one key to another.

Tonality is when a piece of music has a distinct tonic. The tonic may be present for the entire piece, or a composer may choose to modulate the piece to other keys, each having its own tonic. We label this music as "tonal." When you see a title of a piece such as "Sonata in E minor," you know that "e" is the tonic.

Atonality is when a piece of music avoids maintaining a tonic. Atonal music is fairly dissonant.

Chord Progression/Cadence

A **chord progression** is the order in which a series of chords occurs. The harmony of most music relies on chords built upon various notes in a particular scale. Throughout history, certain chord progressions have developed that sound normal to our ears. For instance, think of the bass line at the start of "Summer Lovin'" from *Grease*. The bass line is "T (tonic), T, S (subdominant), S, D (dominant),

D, S, D, S, T" with chords punctuating each note of the bass line—chords built on the tonic, subdominant and dominant. This chord progression is one of the most popular chord progressions in Western music. Most pieces of music from the Classical Era, for example, end with a chord progression of "T, S, D, D, T."

A **cadence** is the last few chords in a chord progression. Ending on the tonic chord provides a sense of conclusion. Cadences occur in music at the ends of phrases as well as the end of the entire piece. Cadences at the ends of compositions often emphasize (repeat) the tonic numerous times to ensure that listeners feel a sense of conclusiveness.

Rhythm

Rhythm is how music occurs within time. At its most basic, rhythm is the succession of *durations* of notes. Some rhythms will feature repeated notes of the same duration, and some rhythms will feature notes with varied durations.

Beat

A **beat** is a regularly recurring pulse. Musical time is measured in "beats." Turn on a rock song with a heavy drumbeat and see what effect it has upon you. Most likely you will start tapping your toe (or banging your head) in a regular, evenly spaced pulse. If you can do that, you have found the beat of the music.

Measure/Bar

A **measure** (or **bar**) is a unit of musical time. Measures are indicated in music by vertical bar lines that look like this:

Meter

Meter is a pattern of regularly recurring accented beats and unaccented beats. There are many different types of meter:

Duple meter: Duple meter is a recurring pattern of one accented beat followed by one unaccented beat—"heavy-light, heavy-light." Most marches by John Philip Sousa are in duple meter.

Triple meter: Triple meter is a recurring pattern of one accented beat followed by two unaccented beats—"heavy-light-light, heavy-light-light." Waltzes and many other dances are in triple meter.

Quadruple meter: Quadruple meter is a recurring pattern of one accented beat followed by a light beat, then a somewhat heavy beat, and then a final light beat—"heavy-light-somewhat heavy-light." This meter is also called "common time" because it is so prevalent in music. Listen to practically any pop song and you will likely hear common time.

Compound meter: Compound meter is a recurring pattern of accented beats and unaccented beats that can be perceived as either duple or triple, and each beat can be subdivided into three beats. As an example of this, sing "Silent Night" faster than you normally would—you'll find that it is in duple meter. Then sing it more slowly, the way it is normally sung and you'll find that it can be perceived in a triple meter:

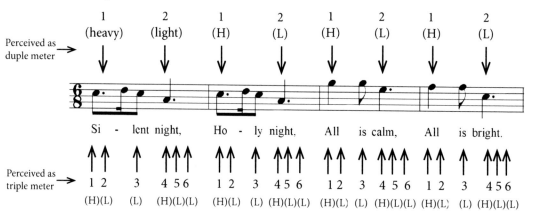

Non-metrical: Some music has no regular recurring pattern of beats, and therefore, no meter. Gregorian chant, for example, is non-metrical.

Mixed meter: Mixed meter is when a piece of music has one meter for a certain amount of time, then shifts to another meter. These shifts can occur every single measure in a piece of music, or infrequently. Listeners might *perceive* pieces composed with mixed meter as nonmetrical, but they are still metrical; the constant shifting makes it more difficult to tap your toes as you listen.

Irregular meter: Irregular meter has an irregular number of beats per measure, for instance, five beats per measure, or seven, or eleven. If a meter isn't easily divisible by two or three, it is irregular.

Texture

Texture is the means by which melody, harmony, and rhythm are combined in a composition.

Monophony: The most basic texture, monophony, is found in music in which a single melody line has absolutely no harmony. Examples of **monophonic texture** in daily life include someone whistling a tune or singing in the shower.

Homophony: This texture is found in music in which a melody line is enhanced or supported by other musical material, usually chords. Examples of **homophonic texture** in daily life include hymns, most pop songs, and patriotic songs.

Polyphony: This texture is found in music in which there are two or more melodic lines that are equal (or practically equal) in importance. There are two main types of **polyphonic texture**:

- **Imitative polyphony** is when one melody line begins and then another melody begins shortly thereafter, imitating the first melody line. The second line might be higher or lower in pitch, or it might use exactly the same pitches as the initial melody, but because the individual entrances are staggered, they are identifiable as separate melodies. There can be as many melodies involved in imitative polyphony as the composer wants. Examples of **imitative polyphonic texture** in daily life include rounds (like *Row, Row, Row Your Boat*) and fugues.
- **Non-imitative polyphony** is when there are two or more contrasting melody lines going on at the same time. Examples of **non-imitative polyphonic texture** include the kids' song, *Fish and Chips and Vinegar*, and "One Day More" from *Les Misérables* (where each character sings his/her own individual melody overlapping with the other characters' individual melodies).

Form

Form refers to the way a particular piece of music is laid out—a "roadmap" or "blueprint" that a composer can follow as he composes a particular piece of music. When diagramming form, letters are used to indicate repetition or contrast. Whatever the first section of music sounds like, it is labeled "A," then, if that first section repeats, it is labeled "A" again. Or if it is contrasting material, it is labeled "B." If another contrasting section occurs, it is labeled "C."

As an example, sing *My Bonnie* and notice how it is diagrammed below:

A	My Bonnie lies over the ocean My Bonnie lies over the sea My Bonnie lies over the ocean Oh, bring back my Bonnie to me
B	Bring back, bring back Oh bring back my Bonnie to me, to me Bring back, bring back Oh bring back my Bonnie to me

The first part is very obviously a different melody than the second part.

Here's an example of a piece in ABA form, or in other words, a piece in which the first section is repeated following a contrasting section. Sing this song aloud and pay attention to how the initial A melody repeats following the B melody.

A	Baa, baa, black sheep, have you any wool? Yes sir, yes sir, three bags full.
B	One for the master, one for the dame, One for the little boy who lives down the lane.
A	Baa, baa, black sheep, have you any wool? Yes sir, yes sir, three bags full.

Note: Diagramming music has nothing to do with the words and everything to do with the melody. In this example, both "A" sections had the same words, but you could also sing the alphabet song and notice that even though the two "A" sections have different words, they should still be diagrammed with "A" because they have the exact same melody.

This next example has no repetition of sections:

A	I've been working on the railroad all the live-long day. I've been working on the railroad just to pass the time away.
B	Can't you hear the whistle blowing, Rise up so early in the morn; Can't you hear the captain shouting, "Dinah, blow your horn!"
C	Dinah, won't you blow, Dinah, won't you blow, Dinah, won't you blow your horn? Dinah, won't you blow, Dinah, won't you blow, Dinah, won't you blow your horn?

D	Someone's in the kitchen with Dinah Someone's in the kitchen I know Someone's in the kitchen with Dinah Strummin' on the old banjo!

Most pop music and rock and roll songs follow a very basic pattern of verse, verse, chorus, verse, chorus—or, in other words, AABAB. Listen to your favorite pop songs and pay attention to the patterns of repetition and contrast present. Occasionally, a section might repeat (A A, for example) but on the repeated part, the composer might have made small changes—not enough to obscure the relationship to the first A, but enough to notice. In these cases, a prime is added to the slightly altered section, like so: A A'.

Movement

A **movement** is a self-contained portion of music (with a beginning, middle, and end) that is part of a larger work. In the example below, the piece listed has a main title followed by four individual movements (indented). Each movement sounds like a complete piece of music. You might even feel like you ought to clap at the end of the first movement (especially if it is particularly exciting), but the first movement is not the end of the complete piece; you need to wait until all four movements are complete before you applaud.

Quintet in D minor, op. 68, no. 3   Franz Danzi
    Andante sostenuto—Allegretto   (1763–1826)
    Andante
    Minuetto: Allegretto
    Finale: Allegro assai

Many music lovers feel that this is a silly rule and others most vociferously defend the practice. In any event, the current concert-going etiquette is to wait until the end of the *entire* piece to applaud. When you attend concerts, follow along with the program to keep track of the movements, so that you know when to applaud.

Score

Score is the word used to describe the printed music of a piece of music. There are solo scores, chamber scores, vocal scores, and orchestral scores.

When studying music it is very helpful to look at scores while you listen. To find scores, the easiest and quickest method is by searching for the composer and title of the piece you are studying at the International Music Score Library

Project's website (imslp.org). Most music libraries at universities also have a tremendous number of scores available.

Repeat Signs

Repeat signs are indications in printed music to show musicians when to repeat sections of the music. They look like two little dots to the right or left of a bar line. Any music located between two repeat signs is what will be repeated by the performer. Here is an example of repeat signs:

Repeat sign   Repeat sign

EXPRESSIVE MARKINGS

Expressive markings are words or symbols that provide guidance to the performer as to how to perform a piece of music. These markings indicate the mood, volume, or speed of the music.

Dynamics

Dynamics are descriptive markings or words printed in the music that indicate volume—how loud or how quiet. Because a lot of musical terms developed at a time when Italy was the artistic center of Europe, we use Italian words to describe dynamics. Dynamics are indicated with various symbols and abbreviations (below the printed notes).

ITALIAN TERM	ENGLISH TRANSLATION	SYMBOL OR ABBREVIATION USED TO INDICATE DYNAMIC
Pianississimo	Triple soft	*ppp*
Pianissimo	Double soft	*pp*
Piano	Soft	*p*
Mezzo-piano	Medium soft	*mp*
Mezzo-forte	Medium loud	*mf*
Forte	Loud	*f*
Fortissimo	Double loud	*ff*
Fortississimo	Triple loud	*fff*

Crescendo	Gradually get louder	*cresc.* or (this symbol is placed underneath a section of music and is as short or as long as the composer wants the crescendo to take place.)
Decrescendo or Diminuendo	Gradually get softer	*decresc.* or *dim.* or
Subito	Suddenly	*sub.* This dynamic marking is only used in conjunction with a specific volume, like so: *sub. fff* or *sub. p*

Dynamics are only general terms. It is up to the individual performer to decide how loud or soft one dynamic is in relation to another dynamic.

Tempo

Tempo is the speed of music. Composers can indicate how fast or how slow a particular piece or section of a piece is by using tempo markings. These are generally in Italian, although other languages are occasionally used. They appear above the printed music at the beginning of the piece and whenever the composer changes the tempo within a piece of music. They also appear in the printed program at music performances, so it is helpful for you to have a working knowledge of these terms. Here is a chart showing the most commonly used tempo markings. While each Italian word has a specific meaning, as long as you understand the general concept, you'll know what to expect when listening to music labeled with these terms.

DESIRED SPEED OF MUSIC	TEMPO MARKINGS COMMONLY USED
Very slow	*Grave, Largo,* and *Lento*
Slow	*Adagio*
Somewhat slow	*Andante* (often translated as "at a walking pace")
Medium speed	*Moderato*
Somewhat fast	*Allegretto*
Fast	*Allegro* and *Vivace* (lively)
Very fast	*Presto*

As with dynamics, these terms are still quite general so it is up to the individual performer to determine how fast or slow each tempo really is. Many composers try to be more specific by using certain modifiers in their tempo markings.

MODIFIER	WHAT IT MEANS	HOW IT MIGHT APPEAR IN CONJUNCTION WITH A TEMPO MARKING
Agitato	Agitated	*Allegro agitato*
Animato	Animated, with life	*Allegro animato*
Appassionato	With passion	*Allegro appassionato*
Assai	Very	*Allegro assai*
Cantabile	In a "singing" manner	*Allegretto cantabile*
Con brio	With vigor	*Allegro con brio*
Con fuoco	With fire	*Presto con fuoco*
Con moto	With motion	*Allegro con moto*
Espressivo	With expressiveness	*Andante espressivo*
Giocoso	With joy	*Allegro giocoso*
Grazioso	With gracefulness	*Allegro grazioso*
Maestoso	Majestic	*Allegro maestoso*
Molto	Much	*Molto allegro*
Non troppo	But not too much	*Allegro non troppo*

The above table is only a sample of the myriad possible terms used as modifiers. If you see a tempo marking that you've never seen before, try using basic knowledge of Latin-based languages (including English) to make educated guesses as to meaning. For instance, one can infer that *Presto furioso* means "fast and furious" or that *Andante sostenuto* means "slow and sustained."

Here are other tempo markings that help guide performers in their music-making:

ITALIAN TERM	ENGLISH TRANSLATION	SYMBOL OR ABBREVIATION USED
Accelerando	Speeding up	*accel.*
Meno mosso	Less motion	*meno mosso*
Più mosso	More motion	*più mosso*
Poco a poco	Little by little	*poco a poco* This term is usually used in conjunction with another tempo marking, for instance, *poco a poco accelerando* would mean "little by little speed up."
Rallentando or Ritardando	Slowing down	*rall.* or *rit.*

Composers can also indicate exact tempo by using metronome markings. A metronome is a time-indicating device that clicks or beeps a certain number of times per minute. As an example, if the metronome marking is "♩ = 60," the click would occur 60 times per minute—a relatively slow tempo. If the metronome marking is "♩ = 176" the click would occur 176 times per minute. On a traditional metronome, 40 is the lowest tempo and 208 is the fastest tempo.

DESCRIPTIVE TERMS

Tone Color/Timbre

Tone color or **timbre** (the terms are interchangeable) is the quality of sound of an instrument or voice. Tone color is affected by the way the sound vibrations are created. To describe tone color, use descriptive adjectives like "smooth," "harsh," "nasal," "mellifluous," or even "toad-like." Sing the exact same pitch multiple times with a different timbre each time; for instance, sing a note with a nasal tone color, then sing the same note with a mellow tone color, then with a gravelly tone color.

Note: Sometimes people make the mistake of describing the mood of a piece when they're trying to describe tone color. Mood and tone color are two different concepts.

Genre

Genre is a word that essentially means the same thing as "category." In music, a genre is a categorical term to help us identify a particular piece of music by characteristics it shares with other compositions.

It might be helpful to illustrate this concept using the world of film as an example. Within the many possibilities of types of films to watch, we find genres such as Comedy, Action, Romance, Horror, Children's Movies, and Westerns. As an example, every film in the "Western" genre shares similar characteristics, the most obvious being that they all take place in the wild West, and they involve gunfights, horses, and saloons. Yet every Western is also uniquely individual. So we use more specific titles within the genre to identify the specific films—*High Noon*; *True Grit*; and *The Wild Bunch* to name a few. Note that although each of these films is easily recognized as a Western, they are each unique.

It works the same way in the world of music. As an example, in music, "concerto" is a specific genre, or category of composition. Individual pieces of music within that genre have more specific titles to help them be identified more specifically than the general term of "genre." As with a Western film, there are hundreds of concertos with unique characteristics and identifying factors with titles such as:

- *Marimba Concerto No. 1*
- *Piano Concerto No. 12 in A major, K. 414*
- *Brandenburg Concerto No. 3 in G major, BWV 1048*
- *The Butterfly Lovers Violin Concerto*

Another example: A genre that originated in the Catholic Church is called "Mass." The Mass is a specific church service; it is also a musical genre that has developed and evolved through the centuries. Within the vast genre of Mass there are hundreds of masses identified more specifically with identifying titles such as:

- *Mass No. 3 in C major, Hob.XXII:5*
- *Mass No. 16 in C major, K. 317, "Krönungsmesse"*
- *Messe solennelle, Op. 16*
- *Mša glagolskaja (Glagolitic Mass), JW III/9*

At some point, you may be asked, "Do you like listening to concertos?" and you might reply in the affirmative, at which point you may be asked, "Which ones?" The person asking you questions has determined that you enjoy the genre of the Mass and now they want more specific titles.

Genre is quite a useful term and can be very broad or very specific. For example, in the world of music one *could* divide up all music that has ever existed into two rather large genres—1) classical music and 2) pop music. These are *extremely* broad genres. Within each of these genres are hundreds of sub-genres. For instance, in the large genre of pop music, there are the sub-genres of R&B, bubble gum pop, country-western, hair metal, and grunge, to name a few, and within the large genre of classical music there are hundreds of sub-genres such as concerto, sonata, symphony, string quartet, and piano trio.

Program Music/Absolute Music

Program music is instrumental music that is meant to tell a story or paint a picture in the head of the listener. **Absolute music** is instrumental music that is *not* meant to tell a story. It is music for music's sake.

Song/Piece

Songs are sung. Songs are usually quite short and are sung by a small number of people (one or two, as opposed to a full choir). It is incorrect to refer to a large-scale composition like Beethoven's *Symphony No. 9* as a song. The word "**piece**" is the general term to use for all other types of compositions.

Pop Music/Art Music

Pop music is music that is "popular." Rock and roll, musical theatre, film music, and jazz are categories of popular music.

Art music is music that is artistic in intent. Classical music from the Middle Ages through the present day is considered art music.

Both terms are problematic. Labeling a piece of music as "pop" implies that it is not artistic; labeling a piece of music as "art music" implies that it is not popular. Neither of those implications is true or fair. Jazz, musical theatre, film music, and rock and roll all have artistic merit. And classical music is indeed "popular" all over the world. For the purposes of this book, however, the terms will be used as indicated above, with the understanding that "pop music" and "art music" are both popular AND artistic.

Instruments and Ensembles

INSTRUMENTS OF CLASSICAL MUSIC

Woodwind Instruments

For all woodwind instruments, pitch is changed by covering and uncovering holes in the body of the instrument and pressing on various keys and buttons.

<u>Flute:</u>

- Flute: Historically, the flute was made of wood; currently, flutes made of metal are standard. The sound is created by blowing across the top of a small opening. To understand how this makes a sound, blow across the top of a bottle and you'll hear how the sound is created.
- Piccolo: The piccolo is a baby flute. It is smaller and therefore plays at a higher pitch.
- Alto flute: This is a larger, and therefore lower, flute. It has a deeper, more breathy tone color than the regular flute.
- Bass flutes and tenor flutes.
- Flutes made of wood, usually from earlier time periods.

<u>Oboe:</u>

- Oboe: The oboe is made of dark wood, and is played by blowing through a small double reed (two pieces of carefully shaped cane strapped back to back).

- English horn: The English horn is essentially a larger oboe. It has a warmer and richer tone color and a lower range.

Clarinet:

- Clarinet: The clarinet is played by blowing on a mouthpiece to which is strapped a single-cane reed. It is made from the same wood as the oboe.
- Bass clarinet: This is a rather large clarinet that looks similar to a saxophone, although it is made of black wood and it rests on the floor.
- E-flat clarinet: This is the baby clarinet. It is high in pitch and has a shrill tone color.
- There are also alto clarinets, contrabass clarinets, and more.

Bassoon:

- Bassoon: The bassoon is a double-reed instrument much larger than the oboe and therefore has a lower pitch and a richer tone color.
- Contrabassoon: This is a huge bassoon that plays very low notes.

Saxophone:

- Alto saxophone: Although it is made of brass, the saxophone is a single-reed instrument (like the clarinet) and shares a similar fingering system with the rest of the woodwinds. This is the most commonly seen and heard saxophone, especially in jazz and pop music. The inventor of the saxophone intended for it to be a regular part of the standard orchestra. Although that never really caught on, hundreds of composers have composed classical repertoire for this instrument.
- Soprano, tenor, baritone, and contra-bass saxophones.

Other Woodwind Instruments:

- Recorder: The recorder is similar to early wood-flutes, but instead of blowing across the top of a hole, sound is produced by blowing through a whistle-type mouthpiece. Because of the focus on recorder in elementary schools, many people do not realize that the recorder is actually a recognized "serious" instrument in the world of classical music. Recorder virtuosi make recordings of concerti by Vivaldi, Corelli, Telemann, and other Baroque composers. The recorder can also be called the *blockflöte* and comes in many varieties such as alto, tenor, and bass.

Brass Instruments

Brass instruments are made of metal tubing that is coiled into various shapes to allow for various tone colors. The length and width of tubing influence how high or low a particular instrument is. All brass instruments produce sound by the performer's buzzing lips pressed into a circular cup-shaped metal mouthpiece. Pitch is influenced by how fast or slow the lips are buzzing, assisted by the use of valves or a slide.

Trumpet:

- Trumpet: The trumpet has a bright, brassy tone color, and uses valves (buttons) that open up passageways to different lengths of mostly cylindrical tubing.
- Cornet: The cornet is very similar to the trumpet in size and method of playing, but has conical tubing and a warmer tone color.
- Flugelhorn: This is very similar to the cornet, but with a darker, warmer tone color.
- Piccolo trumpet: This is the highest trumpet used today. It was extremely popular in the Baroque Era. If you hear a piece of music with a really high trumpet, there is a good possibility that it was composed in the Baroque Era.

Horn; alternatively, French horn:

- Horn: The horn has the mellowest tone color of the brass family and is thus often referred to as an "honorary woodwind." It uses valves (spatula keys) similar to the trumpet, but has a large bell at the end of the tubing into which the performer places the right hand to help influence pitch, volume, and tone color.
- Mellophone: This is basically a horn that has been shaped differently with the bell facing forward. Has a similar tone color to the horn and is used most frequently in marching bands.

Trombone:

- Trombone: The trombone is similar in tone color to the horn, but lower in pitch. Unlike the other brass instruments, the trombone changes pitch using a long slide to extend the tubing. This gives the trombone its unique ability to smear from one note to another smoothly. Some professional models have one or two valves to facilitate note changes.
- There are alto, tenor, and bass varieties.

<u>Tuba:</u>

- Tuba: This is the largest brass instrument standard in a typical orchestra. It has a large bell that points upward and uses valves to change pitch.
- Sousaphone: A tuba designed to be used in marching bands; the bell faces forward to project the sound more directly, and the tubing wraps around the performer for ease of carrying while marching.

String Instruments

The majority of the string family produces sound in a similar way—by drawing a bow (made of horse hair) across four gut or synthetic strings to produce the vibrations. The right hand holds the bow; the left hand places fingers on the fingerboard to create different pitches. The strings can also be plucked (a technique called *pizzicato*). Because the bow can be drawn across more than one string at a time, string instruments can often play both melody and harmony at the same time. Playing two strings at once is a technique known as "double stops." String players also use a technique known as *vibrato* in which the left hand wiggles back and forth, which causes a slight change in pitch repeatedly.

<u>Violin:</u>

- The violin is the smallest of the standard orchestral strings and is held under the chin. It can have a bright, thin tone color in its highest notes and a warm, mellow tone color on its lower notes.

<u>Viola:</u>

- The viola is slightly larger than the violin and has a warm, dark tone color.

<u>Cello:</u>

- Also referred to as a "violoncello," this is a larger instrument that looks similar to the violin and viola, but instead of being played by being held under the chin, it is placed on the floor between the legs of the performer. It has a lower pitch and a darker tone color than the viola.

<u>Double-bass:</u>

- This is the largest string instrument. Performers of the double-bass (also called "string bass," "upright bass," or "bass") either stand while playing or sit on a tall stool.

<u>Other String Instruments:</u> These other instruments are considered string instruments because the principal creation of the sound is the vibrations of strings; these instruments are not bowed, but are instead strummed or plucked.

- Guitar: The guitar has six strings and, although endemic in pop music, its origins are classical; there is a vast classical repertoire for the guitar.
- Harp: The harp has a large wood soundboard with up to 47 strings. Professional harps have seven pedals at the base that have three positions—natural, lowered, and raised—by which the performer can change keys. There are also less-complex harps for beginners and Celtic harps used mostly in folk music.

Percussion Instruments

A percussion instrument is any instrument in which the principal means of producing sound is by striking the instrument. Some percussion instruments are pitched, meaning they produce a specific note that could be matched on the piano keyboard, and others are un-pitched, meaning that the vibrations produced are not regular enough to create a specific pitch (stomp your foot and you will hear an un-pitched sound).

- Timpani: A set of pitched instruments, also known as the kettledrums, timpani are placed in a half-circle of four to six separate drums of different sizes. The performer sits in the middle of the half circle for ease of access to each drum. Each timpani also has a foot pedal by which the performer can change pitch.
- Glockenspiel: Pitched. A glockenspiel is laid out with two rows of metal bars containing all the pitches of the chromatic scale. To strike the bars, performers use hard rubber or wood mallets.
- Xylophone: Pitched. The xylophone is extremely similar to a glockenspiel, but with wood bars and lower in pitch.
- Vibraphone: Pitched. Similar to a glockenspiel, but much larger with metal tubes underneath each bar to help the sound resonate and "ring." Inside the metal tubes is a rotating disc that creates a very regular vibrato effect. There is also a damper pedal to muffle the sound.
- Marimba: Pitched. The marimba is similar to the vibraphone, but with wood bars and no rotating discs.
- Chimes: Pitched. Chimes are metal tubes that hang vertically from a frame and are struck at the top with a hammer. There is also a damper pedal similar to a vibraphone.
- Snare drum: Un-pitched. A snare drum is a small drum struck with wood drumsticks. There are metal springs, called snares, stretched out along the

bottom of the drum, which create a rattle when the drum is struck. Think of the beginning of practically any military march—usually the first sounds you hear are produced by the snare drum.

- Tambourine: Un-pitched. The tambourine is a wooden hoop with metal discs loosely inset all around the hoop to rattle against each other when struck.
- Castanets: Un-pitched. Castanets look like two really short, fat, shallow wooden spoons tied together with the indented parts facing each other. They are held with one "spoon" in the palm of the hand and the fingers strike the back of the other "spoon" to clack them together. In orchestral settings, castanets are often mounted for ease of playing. Often used in music with a Spanish influence.
- Triangle: Un-pitched. A metal triangle struck with a metal beater.
- Cymbals: Un-pitched. Usually two metal concave brass discs struck together for a ringing effect. There are also suspended cymbals, which are single cymbals that can be struck with mallets for various effects. Do an online search for "how cymbals work" to see the many varieties of sounds that can be created.
- Gong: Pitched. Gongs are metal discs of many different sizes struck with mallets.
- Tam-Tam: Un-pitched. A tam-tam is a large metal disc struck with a large mallet.
- Bass drum: Un-pitched. A really big drum, struck with a large mallet. Marching bands usually include a bass drum line with bass drums of various sizes and pitches.
- There are many other drums and percussive instruments not described including tenor drums, bongos, congas, tom-toms, cowbells, steel-pans, slapsticks, ethnic drums, and household items.

Keyboard Instruments

- Piano: The standard keyboard instrument. Many varieties, but mainly upright (used in domestic or classroom settings) and "grand" (used in professional venues). The sound is created when the performer strikes the keys on the keyboard. Each key activates a felt-tipped hammer inside the body of the instrument, which strikes a string. Because of this, pianos are often classified as percussion instruments. There are also pedals to allow the sound to resonate, or to muffle the sound. When the piano was first invented it was called a *pianoforte* because it could play at both the *piano* level of dynamic and the *forte* level of dynamic (and all dynamics in between) depending on how hard the performer struck the keys.
- Organ: Seen most often in churches and concert halls, the organ produces sound in a different way than the piano. Each key on the keyboard is attached

by airways to a different sized pipe. In addition, most organs have multiple keyboards stacked one above the other. The performer also usually has access to panels on each side of the keyboard covered with little knobs or switches called "stops." Each stop is connected to a different set of pipes. Sets of pipes vary in shape—round or square, flared or tapered—and materials—different kinds of metal and wood—to create a huge variety of tone colors. By pulling a stop out, the performer opens up the airway to that particular set of pipes. If a performer pulls all the stops out, air is being sent to all the pipes. If you've ever heard the phrase "I'm pulling out all the stops tonight!" you now know where it comes from. Performers can also pre-assign certain stops to certain keyboards. The right hand might be playing on the lowest-positioned keyboard using the brass-sounding sets of pipes, while the left hand could be playing on the next keyboard up with the stops set to the wood pipes for a more flute-like sound. Being trained as an organist is quite different from being trained as a pianist because, in addition to using both hands, organists also use their feet to play another "keyboard" at the base of the organ.

- Harpsichord: The predecessor to the piano. Instead of activating felt hammers—like the piano—when a performer strikes the keys of a harpsichord, each key activates a small hook, or "plectrum" that plucks the string. This produces a tinny, brittle tone color. If you hear a harpsichord, the composition is most likely from the Baroque Era.
- Celesta or celeste: The celesta is a glockenspiel in a case with a piano keyboard. When the performer strikes the keys on the keyboard, mallets strike the glockenspiel. The celesta sounds almost identical to the glockenspiel but has the added advantage of being able to produce as many pitches at a time as there are fingers on the performer.
- Synthesizer: An electronic instrument, the synthesizer is most frequently heard in pop music.

Voice Types

- Soprano: This is the highest female voice. The typical range of a soprano is from middle C (on the piano keyboard) and to two octaves above middle C.
- Mezzo-soprano: This is the next-highest female voice. The typical range of a mezzo soprano is an interval of a third below the soprano.
- Alto: This is generally the lowest female voice. The typical range of an alto is an interval of a third below the mezzo-soprano.
- Boy soprano: Same range as soprano, but a different tone color. Usually boy sopranos have a more glassy tone color and use less (or no) vibrato.
- Countertenor: A high male voice, approximately the same range as a female alto. The countertenor voice can be a falsetto voice or a "true"

voice, meaning the vocal cords have been carefully trained to sing in that range.

- Tenor: The most common high male voice. The typical range is about a fifth below an alto.
- Baritone: The middle male voice. Typical range is about a third below a tenor.
- Bass: The low male voice. The typical range is about a third below a baritone.

ENSEMBLES OF CLASSICAL MUSIC

The word "**ensemble**" means "group." The following are the main ensembles common in the world of classical music.

Instrumental Ensembles

Orchestra

An **orchestra** is a large ensemble that features mostly string instruments. Depending on the time period, the number of woodwind, brass, percussion, and keyboard instruments varies widely. Orchestras are sometimes called "Symphony Orchestra" or "Symphony" for short; they are also sometimes called "Philharmonic" or "Philharmonia."

Baroque Orchestra

In the Baroque Era, the orchestra varied widely in size based mainly on what instruments were available. Some Baroque orchestral works were composed for as few as seven instrumentalists, while other orchestral works call for over 80 instruments. The standard Baroque orchestra likely had three or four 1st violins (all playing the same part), three or four 2nd violins, three or four violas, one or two cellos, one doublebass, and one keyboard instrument, most likely harpsichord or organ. Depending on the composer (and possibly the person who commissioned the composition) there may be various woodwind, brass, and percussion instruments. The woodwind instruments that were available in the Baroque Era were flutes, oboes, and bassoons; brass instruments were trumpet and horn; and percussion was timpani.

Classical Orchestra

In the Classical Era, the orchestra became much more standardized in size, and all the different instrument families were represented. Strings: six 1st violins, six 2nd violins, four violas, two cellos, one or two double-bass. Woodwinds: two flutes, two oboes, two clarinets, two bassoons. Brass: two trumpets, two to four horns (less common, but occasionally trombones and tuba were used). Percussion: timpani and various other bells and cymbals (but not too many).

Romantic Orchestra

In the Romantic Era, the orchestra grew considerably in size. Strings: at least double the number used in the previous time period. Woodwinds: two flutes, one piccolo; two oboes, one English horn; two clarinets, one bass clarinet; two bassoons, one contrabassoon (and, depending on the composer, sometimes the woodwinds were increased even more, including a new instrument, the saxophone). Brass: two trumpets; four horns; two tenor trombones, one bass trombone; and tuba (and again, depending on composer, sometimes the brass were increased even more). Percussion: timpani, snare drum, bass drum, gong, cymbals of all varieties, castanets, triangle, chimes, xylophone.

Twentieth-Century Orchestra and Contemporary Orchestra

From the twentieth century onward, when it comes to which instruments belong in the orchestra, truly anything goes. Electronic instruments, car horns, and manipulated recordings are all fair game in modern music.

Pit Orchestra

A pit orchestra is used in the classical genres of opera and ballet. It is located in a "pit" in front of (and lower than) the stage, or partially underneath the stage. Pit orchestras vary in size and instrumentation depending on the time period.

Wind Ensemble

Also referred to as "wind symphony," "concert band," and "symphonic band," wind ensembles feature woodwind, brass, and percussion instruments. Because there are no strings involved (except for a lone double-bass or harp on occasion) all the woodwind and brass instruments are in greater numbers than you would find in an orchestra. For example, instead of the two or three clarinets you would find in a typical orchestra, there could be up to twenty in a wind ensemble. Wind ensembles often play transcriptions or arrangements of orchestral repertoire, but there is an increasing number of compositions composed specifically for the wind ensemble.

Chamber Music

Chamber music refers to ensembles of a smaller size than an orchestra, usually a group of between two and twenty performers. Numerous combinations are possible—duo, trio, quartet, quintet, sextet, septet, octet, nonet, dectet, hendectet, and more. Among the most common are

- Piano Trio (usually violin, cello, piano)
- String Quartet (usually two violins, one viola, one cello)
- Piano Quintet (string quartet and piano)
- Wind Quintet (flute, oboe, clarinet, bassoon, French horn)
- Brass Quintet (two trumpets, trombone, French horn, tuba)

Chamber music is so called because originally, music written for these smaller ensembles was intended to be performed in someone's chamber, or, in other words, in his/her living room. Louis XIV, for instance, would have court musicians perform not only in his living room chamber, but in his bed chamber to wake him in the morning, in his dining chamber while he ate meals, and, disturbingly, in his bath chamber.

Exceptions to the above: The above definition focuses on pieces of music composed for between two and twenty performers. But the piano sonatas of the Classical Era and character pieces of the Romantic Era—composed for a solo piano—were also intended to be performed in a chamber and can therefore be considered "chamber music."

Vocal Ensembles

- **Chorus** is a vocal ensemble that generally specializes in secular music.
- **Choir** is a vocal ensemble that generally specializes in sacred music.

FURTHER INVESTIGATION: Get to know the sounds of each of the main instruments used in classical music. Work your way through the list above methodically finding recordings or videos online featuring each of these instruments in a classical setting. A simple keyword search of the name of the instrument will yield many recordings. For some instruments, such as saxophone, that are better known for their use in jazz or pop music, you may need to modify your keyword search thusly: "classical saxophone." For each instrument, find and listen to as many recordings as you need to ensure that you will recognize the sound of each instrument. (Note: For many instruments, such as the piano, you may be able to identify its sound without listening to any examples.)

Attending Concerts

Concert Etiquette

Attending a professional musical performance should always be a fun and fulfilling experience. It can also be a daunting or disorienting experience if you are unaware of the generally accepted concert etiquette. This is similar to attending a sporting event for the first time. As soon as the attendee becomes aware of expected behavioral norms, the experience is much more enjoyable.

Arriving: Do everything in your power to arrive on time. If you are late, do not walk to your seat during a piece of music. Wait until you hear applause; you may then enter without interrupting the actual performance. At some venues, you may enter between movements of a particular piece. But whatever you do, once you're in the hall, do everything in your power to get to your seat swiftly and quietly. Do not be a distraction to the rest of the audience.

Leaving: Do not leave during a piece of music. Wait until there is applause; you may then leave without interrupting the actual performance. Exceptions to this include uncontrollable coughing or if you are having a medical emergency—in those cases, please leave as swiftly as possible to ensure your health.

Behavior: During a musical performance, you should not make any noise. Keep in mind that music performances are truly the live creation of art. If you make noise during a musical performance it is akin to wiping your hand across the wet canvas of a professional artist. Here are just *some* of the noises that could disturb people sitting near you:

- Opening crinkly candy wrappers—If you must have candy or a cough drop, wait to unwrap it until there is applause.
- Talking—Even if you think you can whisper really softly, everyone in the room—including the performers on stage—can still hear your "esses."
- Coughing/Sneezing—If you need to cough, do everything in your power to hold it in until the end of the piece or movement. Sneezes sometimes catch you off guard, but if you feel one coming on, pinch the bridge of your nose or press against your top lip. And if all else fails and you *have* to sneeze or cough, shove your face as firmly into your inner elbow as possible to muffle the noise.
- Clicking pens—Many people have a habit of clicking their pens without even realizing that they are doing it. Don't be that person.
- Using electronic devices—It is inappropriate to use electronic devices. The light from the device distracts those sitting behind you. Plus, no matter how softly you think you can type on a keyboard, the little clicks can still be heard throughout the hall.
- Cellphones—Turn your cellphones completely off. Cell phone signals can interfere with recording devices.
- Tapping feet—It's noisy. Don't do it.
- Young children—If you bring young children with you, keep them silent throughout the performance. In general, it is considered inappropriate to bring children younger than six years old, and, depending on the maturity level of the child, perhaps not even younger than twelve years old. Some performance venues have minimum age requirements.

When is it appropriate to clap? You can clap at the end of a piece of music. Do not clap after a single movement of a multi-movement work—wait until all the movements have occurred before clapping. And please wait until the piece of music is truly *over* before clapping. There are occasionally people in the audience who desire so badly to be the first person to clap that they start clapping during the final note of a piece. If the conductor's arms are still up, or if the performers instruments are still in playing position, don't clap. Exceptions: In ballet, you may clap *during* the music if the dancer(s) did something particularly praise-worthy. In opera, you can clap after arias or choruses, and, of course, at the end of each scene or act.

When is it appropriate to yell things? There are only certain things you should yell at a music performance, and *only* during applause.

- You may yell "encore" if you want the performers to perform again.

- You may yell "bravo" if you loved the performance and clapping isn't expressive enough. (If you want to be technically correct, yell "bravo" if the performer is a man, "brava" if the performer is a woman, and "bravi" if you are cheering for multiple performers.)
- Even the "woo!" sound, once reserved for less formal occasions, is becoming increasingly common (and perfectly acceptable) in classical music venues.
- You may even yell "boo" if you truly thought the performance was atrocious, but be prepared for angry looks from people sitting near you.

When is it appropriate to give a standing ovation? Give a standing ovation only when you were swept away by the music to such an extent that mere clapping is not enough to show your joy. Standing ovations are also a nice way to show that you would like to hear an encore number.

How to dress: This depends entirely on the venue. If you are paying to see a professional ensemble perform, dress up. If you are attending a performance on a college campus and you don't have time to go home between your last class and the performance, go as you are. Performers would rather have you there than not. You will see people dressed formally and informally at practically every venue. On opening night at the ballet or the opera, or the start of an orchestra's season, you will see people dressed in full tuxedos and evening gowns, as well as a few people in jeans.

Things to Look for at a Performance

Obtain a program and read it: Programs contain lots of helpful information and can actually make your experience much more exciting. The essential elements listed in the program can help you understand what you are about to hear. For instance, as you learn more about the genres, styles, and forms of the different time periods, you will recognize certain terms as part of titles. Then, when you read a title of a piece listed in the program you will have at least a small idea of what you're about to hear. Next to each title, you will find the name of the composer and his/her birth (and death) date. This helps you pinpoint the time period in which the piece was written. As you learn about historical compositional characteristics, even a birth date can help you know something about what you are about to hear. Some performing arts organizations will even include program notes in the printed program. Program notes are detailed descriptions of the pieces you are going to hear.

Watch the performers/conductor: You can gain a lot from attending a music performance simply by watching the performers exhibit their emotions and passion as they perform. Singers, particularly, are very expressive both with facial expressions and physical movement in their efforts to share the emotion or the storyline of the piece they are performing. When pianists or other instrumentalists make huge physical gestures during a performance, they are not merely posturing or acting; in most cases, they are often unaware of their physicality—they are allowing the music to move them as they perform.

Meet the performers: Depending on the venue, it may or may not be appropriate to go backstage to talk to the performers, but if you have the opportunity, take advantage of it. Performers appreciate hearing how the music moved you. They want to know that what they are doing is of value to the listeners.

MIDDLE AGES (450-1450)

The Middle Ages featured sacred and secular music. The majority of written music preserved from the Middle Ages was sacred. The clergy were educated and literate; as a result, they were able to write the music down so future listeners could enjoy it. In addition, the way music was performed in the Catholic Church lent itself to preservation because it was passed down from generation to generation.

Instruments in the Middle Ages

None of the instruments common today existed in the Middle Ages. There were earlier versions of flutes, recorders, violins, guitars and trombones, but they were not called by those names. For instance, the medieval trombone was called a sackbut.

Performance Venues in the Middle Ages

Many of the performance venues common today did not exist in the Middle Ages. For instance, there was no such thing as a concert hall, recital hall or opera house. The two most important performance venues in the Middle Ages were the church and the court. The church was an important performance venue due to the large amount of music used in church services such as the Mass. Music was also performed frequently in the homes of the nobility by court musicians as well as by the nobility themselves.

Compositional and Performance Techniques of the Middle Ages

Performance Technique: *A cappella* Singing

A *cappella* is singing that is not accompanied by musical instruments. The term *a cappella* literally means "to the chapel" or "in the style of the chapel" because early church music was sung without instrumental accompaniment.

Genres that feature *a cappella* singing:

- Mass
- Motets
- Organa
- Plainchant
- Troubadour songs

Exceptions to the definition above: Occasionally, performers would add musical instruments to their performances.

Compositional Technique: Church Modes

A **mode** is a scale. Before the development of the major/minor scale system that we use today, there were a number of modes that were used in the Middle Ages. They each sound somewhat similar to the major/minor scales we use today, but the order of half steps and whole steps is different enough to make them sound somewhat foreign to us. It was believed, at the time, that the modes could influence the way the listener felt and/or behaved. As a result, the Catholic Church approved only certain modes for use in the church. It felt that certain modes were more likely to turn the listener's minds toward heaven and other modes were more likely to lead to sin. This may strike a modern person as simplistic or silly, but in reality, most of us would readily agree that we listen to certain kinds of music when in a good mood and other kinds of music when in a bad mood.

Genres that used church modes: All the sacred genres. Modes are still used today by composers who are striving to achieve a certain sound. They are also used in jazz music.

Performance Technique: Drone

A **drone** is a sustained, continuous pitch. Drones could be produced by a string instrument, a wind instrument, or a very basic table top organ (organs in the Middle Ages were simple keyboards—not at all like the keyboards of today—with one pipe per key and a small bellows to provide air for the pipes). Drones are still used in music today in period ensembles, bagpipe music, and some contemporary compositions.

Genres that used a drone:

- Plainchants—Performers started using drones along with chants sometime in the middle of the Middle Ages.
- Many secular genres used drones.

Compositional Technique: Isorhythm

Isorhythm is a recurring rhythm. It was usually used in the lowest sung line of medieval motets. Although the rhythm repeated, the note patterns did not—same rhythm, different melody. As a result, it takes a discerning ear to actually be aware of the presence of isorhythm. It is helpful to have the printed music in front of you to see it visually. At first, composers would use isorhythm in only one line, but as time went on, composers started using isorhythm in multiple lines, and in some cases, all lines.

Genres of the Middle Ages

Mass

In the Catholic Church there are many possible church services each day. Arguably, the most important of these is the **Mass**.

The Mass, and what determines the text/music used each day, is fairly complex, but the basic components that you should understand are as follows:

Certain texts within the Mass change from day to day depending on which "feast day" it is on the church calendar. Feast days are usually associated with particular Saints or events in the life of Christ. There are also Masses for purposes such as funerary rites, known as Requiem Masses. The texts that change from day to day are known as **Proper** texts.

There are other texts that are the same every time you attend Mass. These texts are known as **Ordinary** texts. The five sections of the Mass in which the texts stay the same are 1) Kyrie, 2) Gloria, 3) Credo, 4) Sanctus, and 5) Agnus Dei.

Historically, composers spent more time and effort on creating elaborate music for the Ordinary sections of the Mass, whereas the Proper sections were simpler. For instance, in the Middle Ages, the Proper sections featured simple recitation (see "plainchant") and the Ordinary sections featured much more intricate music, perhaps with larger intervals, and maybe even polyphony. The reason composers did this was that the text used for the Proper was used only on that specific day each year (if at all) whereas the text for the Ordinary was used daily.

Composers, therefore, hoping for their music to be heard more frequently, leaned toward setting the texts that were heard more frequently. The Mass continues to be a vital part of the Catholic Church service, and, therefore, is a vital music genre.

Performing forces: *A cappella* voices. At some point, drones were introduced, possibly to help the singers stay on pitch, possibly to reflect the homophonic texture of some secular music. The large pipe organs to which we have become accustomed did not exist in the Middle Ages.

FURTHER INVESTIGATION:

1. Attend a Catholic Mass. If available, obtain a printed program so you can look for the Ordinary sections of the Mass. Notice the texture of the different sections of the Mass to see if the Ordinary sections are more elaborate than the Proper sections. It is likely that masses you attend will have a variety of musical examples from different time periods.
2. Listen to a Mass composed in the Middle Ages. Notice the texture of the different sections of the Mass to see if the Ordinary sections are more elaborate than the Proper sections.

SUGGESTED LISTENING: Any music from a Middle Ages Mass. Search online for keywords "Gregorian chant," "Codex Sanblasianus" or "Liber Usualis."

Plainchant

Plainchant—also known as "Gregorian" chant, plainsong, or, simply, chant—was the main type of music heard in the Catholic Church for the first half of the Middle Ages. Most of the music in the Mass—as well as the other daily church services—was plainchant. The main characteristics of chant are

- monophonic—no harmony
- non-metrical—no regular sense of pulse
- modal—composed using church modes
- Latin text—there is one Ordinary text in the Mass—the Kyrie—which is in Greek, but the rest of the Mass is in Latin. Note: In the mid-1960's the Catholic Church changed policy and allowed the High Mass to be sung in the language of the country in which it was performed.

Plainchant flourished from the beginning of the Middle Ages through about the year 900 when polyphonic compositions began to evolve.

Compositional techniques used in plainchant:

- **Syllabic** text settings —text settings in which there is one note per syllable.
- **Neumatic** text settings—text settings in which there are a few notes per syllable.
- **Melismatic** text settings—text settings in which there are a lot of notes per syllable.

General types of plainchant: There are many different kinds of plainchant. The main types are

- **Recitation**—chant in which one pitch is dominant throughout with only small deviations from the pitch at the beginning of the phrase or at the cadence. These chants can be quite monotonous, but can also be hypnotic and calming.
- **Responsory**—chant in which a "call and response" is heard between one singer and a group of singers, or sometimes between two separate groups of singers.
- **Non-responsory**—chants in which there is no "call and response" effect.

Other words you might see in a printed program at a Mass service (with its definition):

- Alleluia —melismatic responsorial plainchant
- Antiphon —responsorial plainchant with melismas at the cadences or occasionally to embellish a word or phrase.
- Gradual —highly melismatic plainchant
- Introit —the first thing you'll hear at a Mass. It is the introductory antiphon.
- Sequence—non-responsorial syllabic plainchants (with small neumatic moments) with an AA BB CC DD etc. form.
- Tract—non-responsorial, mainly neumatic and syllabic plainchant, with melismas at the cadences.
- Trope—a technique by which extra liturgical phrases were added to other texts. If an Ordinary section had tropes added, it was no longer Ordinary, it was Proper.

About halfway through the Middle Ages, performers started adding a drone to their performances of plainchant.

Even up to the present day, plainchants from the Middle Ages are still performed in church services. Composers in later time periods composed plainchants as well, although not nearly as many as in the Middle Ages.

FURTHER INVESTIGATION:

1. Attend a Catholic Church service. Try to find a Catholic Church that has a good choir. Pay attention to how much recitation you hear versus neumatic or melismatic chants. After the Middle Ages, when homophonic music was the norm, resourceful composers wrote organ accompaniment or other harmonies to the original plainchants, so you may hear a blend of new and old when you attend a church service.
2. Pick a chant from the list above (for example, "Alleluia" or "Introit") and listen to or watch five or six of them online to see if you can identify their chief characteristics as listed above.
3. Search online for a scanned version of the *Liber Usualis* (a collection of chants following the church calendar). Near the start of the book, there are illustrated instructions on how to read the older style of writing music. Using your newfound knowledge, turn to the section in the book with all the chants and try to sing a few.

SUGGESTED LISTENING:

- Anonymous—Since most church composers chose to remain anonymous (to give the glory to God), do a keyword search for "chant" or "plainchant" or "Gregorian chant" or "Liber Usualis."
- Hildegard von Bingen's *Ordo virtutum*
- Notker Balbulus' *Gaude Maria virgo*

Organa/Organum

Around the middle of the Middle Ages (900), an interesting development took place in church music—the addition of polyphonic compositions to the church service. These compositions are called **organa** (organum in the singular). To compose an organum, composers took a pre-existing chant and then wrote a new melodic line to be sung at the same time as the pre-existing chant. This second melody could be written either above or below the chant. Both voice parts sang the same syllables at the same time.

At first organa were composed in parallel motion. In other words, if the notes in the pre-existing chant were ascending or descending, the notes in the new melody did the same. As composers became accustomed to this early polyphony, they began composing in a blend of parallel motion and contrary motion. In other words, if the notes in the chant were ascending, the notes in the new melody could be ascending as well (parallel motion) or descending (contrary motion). An organum in which the pre-existing chant was joined by one new melody was called an "organum duplum."

After a while, composers started adding *more* than one new melody to create an "organum triplum" or "organum quadruplum." They could add as many new melodies to the original chant as they wanted, but again, all the voices had to sing the same syllables at the same time.

As composers continued exploring this new genre, organa started to have each voice sing different numbers of syllables. For instance, one voice might be singing one syllable on a sustained pitch while another voice sang the same syllable in a lengthy melisma.

Over time, composers relegated the original chant to the lowest part and sustained each note for a long time—almost like a drone. The new voices, on the other hand, were full of melismas. The compositional interest was most certainly located in the new voices, not the pre-existing chant.

<u>Performing forces:</u> *A cappella* voices. When the original chant was stretched out into really long notes, sometimes the human voice would be replaced by a drone. But in general, organa were performed *a cappella*.

FURTHER INVESTIGATION: Search online for "organum" and listen to five different organa (audio or video). Try to determine at what stage in the development outlined above each organum is.

SUGGESTED LISTENING:

- Léonin's *Notum fecit Dominus salutare suum ante conspectum gentium revelavit justitiam suam* (organum duplum)
- Perotin's *Viderunt omnes fines terre salutare dei nostri jubilate deo omnis terra* (organum quadruplum)

Troubadour Songs

Most of the written music we have from the Middle Ages was written down by educated members of the clergy. We don't have much secular music because most of the secular composers were illiterate; they couldn't write it down to preserve it. The secular music that we *do* have was composed by people who could afford an education. The types of people who fall into this category are 1) members of the nobility and 2) educated musicians who worked in the homes of the wealthy as their personal, in-house composers. Music was a common hobby among the nobility and many were trained in the art of music performance and composition. These composers were referred to as **troubadours**, trobairitz, trouvères, and Minnesingers, depending on in what region of Europe they lived. For ease of explanation, the "catch-all" term *troubadour* will be used. Note: Sometimes people picture troubadours as wandering minstrels, traveling from town to town performing music for money. This was only partially true. The troubadours would certainly travel about, but mainly to work for an extended period of time for a new employer.

The subject matter of troubadour songs was most often secular; songs about glorious battles or knights saving princesses, or drinking songs, and the most popular topic of secular songs—love and/or lust. In fact, it is sometimes surprising for modern ears to hear the words to certain secular songs from the Middle Ages and realize how ribald they were.

Performing forces: Performing forces depended on 1) the composer's personal preferences, 2) which instruments were available, and 3) who the singer was. But a good generalization is a solo singer. Occasionally, there may have been some string or wind accompaniment (or maybe both) and occasionally a basic drum to provide some rhythm. But unlike the fully formed chords used in modern secular music as a harmonic support to the melody, the accompaniment to troubadour songs was often one or two notes played in an alternating rhythmic pattern. Also, sometimes a solo instrument would play the melody at the same time as the singer.

Types of troubadour songs: This is only a small sampling of the many sub-genres within the genre of troubadour songs.

- Alba —An alba is a song about two lovers parting as the sun rises, often warned by a friend standing guard of the approach of one or both of their spouses.
- Escondig —a song in which a man apologizes to a lady for his inappropriate behavior.
- Gab —a bragging song.
- Pastorela—a song about a knight encountering a shepherd girl and the results of such a meeting. These could be bawdy or comical in nature.
- Planh —a mourning song at the death of royalty.
- Salut d'amour —a love letter song

Over time, troubadour songs developed into other types of secular songs; the term "troubadour songs" was no longer used. Interestingly enough, it is quite common for today's pop artists (particularly folk rock and indie rock) to be referred to as "modern-day troubadours."

Period ensembles continue to perform music from the Middle Ages at formal concerts, Renaissance fairs, Shakespearean festivals, and similar events throughout the world. There are radio and online programs that exclusively feature music of the Middle Ages. Films that are set in the Middle Ages, or even in a fantasy world that resembles the Middle Ages (like *Lord of the Rings*), often use actual troubadour songs, or have songs within the film that are inspired by or that try to mimic the sound of troubadour songs.

FURTHER INVESTIGATION: Search online for any of the sub-genres of troubadour songs listed above.

SUGGESTED LISTENING:

- Bernart de Ventadorn's *Lanquan vei la folha*
- Bernger von Horheim's *Nu enbeiz ich doch des trankes nie*
- Moniot d'Arras' *Ce fut en mai*

Exceptions to the definition above: There were some troubadour songs that were religious in nature. Usually they dealt with efforts to avoid sin, and to express the joy of repentance and the goodness of God. Despite the sacred subject matter, these were not performed in church.

Motet

The **motet** in the Middle Ages is composed in almost exactly the same manner as an organum; in other words, composers would take a pre-existing plainchant, then add to it one or more new melodic lines. Unlike organa, however, each vocal line had its own unique text. The motet began as a sacred genre, with each added melody line featuring either liturgical text or a poem about a sacred matter.

This compositional technique created a unique challenge to the listener, namely that of comprehension. When two or three vocal lines were occurring at the same time with two or three separate texts, it became quite cluttered-sounding.

At some point in the Middle Ages, composers began using non-sacred texts for the additional melody lines, which made the motet even more unusual—multiple texts, some sacred, some secular, all overlapping at the same time.

Note: In the Renaissance, the motet developed in another direction, returning to its sacred roots and abandoning the compositional technique used in the Middle Ages.

Performing forces: Most often, motets were performed *a cappella*. Occasionally, the original plainchant was performed by an instrument (for the same reasons as in organa).

Compositional technique used in motets: Isorhythm.

FURTHER INVESTIGATION:

1. Look at a score of a motet from the Middle Ages. Take note of the multiple texts used (one text per vocal line). If the translations of the text are provided, see if you can determine which texts are sacred and which are secular. Look at the bottom line to see if you can find an example of isorhythm.
2. Listen to motets (make sure they're from the Middle Ages) to take note of how cluttered the multiple texts can sound and to see if you can hear the isorhythm. This would be most effective if you have the score in hand so you can follow along as you listen.

SUGGESTED LISTENING:

- Guillaume de Machaut's *Fias volontas tua/Qui plus aimme/Aucune gent*
- John Dunstable's *Gaude virgo salutata/Gaude virgo singularis/Virgo mater comprobaris/Ave gemma, JD 28*
- Philippe de Vitry's *Trahunt in precipicia/Quasi non ministerium/Ve qui gregi*

Composers of the Middle Ages

Anonymous

Many composers of the Middle Ages chose to remain anonymous. This may have been because church composers were members of holy orders (monks and nuns) composing music with the express purpose of glorifying God; to avoid the sin of pride, they remained anonymous. In secular genres, composers at first attached their names to their compositions, but as time went on, composers who were members of the nobility felt that composing was a lowly profession and didn't want to be seen doing something below their station.

Hildegard of Bingen (1098–1179)

Country: Germany
Interesting facts:

- Was the tenth child of her parents, and was subsequently *tithed* to the church when she was a young girl and became a nun (sources vary on what age—anywhere from eight to fourteen).
- Had visions throughout her life, including as a young child.
- Wrote a number of books on a wide range of topics including science, medicine, religion, and her visions.

- Has been referred to as a saint for a very long time, but her sainthood was made official only quite recently—by Pope Benedict XVI in October of 2012.

Best known for:

- Genre: plainchant
- Composition: *Ordo Virtutum (Play of the Virtues)*—a liturgical drama about the struggle for the human soul between the devil and the virtues.

Highly recommended: *Columba aspexit*

Walther von der Vogelweide (c. 1170–c. 1230)

Country: Germany
Interesting facts:

- Not much is known about his life.
- From the writings of poets and musicians of the time, it is clear that he was held in the highest esteem as both a poet and composer.

Best known for:

- Genre: secular songs, particularly Minnesang (similar to troubadour songs)
- Composition: Due to the notation system used and the way the music was transmitted over time, many melodies by Vogelweide may have been altered over the years.

Highly recommended: *Unter der linden an der heide*

Other Composers

NAME	DATES	COUNTRY	GENRE
Arras, Moniot d'	c. 1200–1240	France	Trouvère songs
Balbulus, Notker	c. 840–912	Switzerland	Plainchant (text)
Dunstable, John	c. 1385–1450	England	Masses, isorhythmic motets
Halle, Adam de la	c. 1235–1285	France	Trouvère songs
Landini, Francesco	c. 1325–1395	Italy	Sacred and secular
Léonin	c. 1150–1200	France	Organa
Machaut, Guillaume de	c. 1300–1375	France	Sacred and secular
Perotin	c. 1160–c. 1215	France	Organa
Ventadorn, Bernart de	c. 1135–c. 1195	France	Troubadour songs
Vitry, Philippe de	1291–1361	France	Sacred and secular
Wolkenstein, Oswald von	c. 1375–1445	Germany	Minnesang (secular songs)

RENAISSANCE ERA (1400-1600)

The Renaissance Era was a time of increased educational opportunities for the general public. The development of the printing press enabled music to be purchased by the average citizen and distributed much more easily. Music in the Renaissance was influenced by the popularity of polyphonic writing for the human voice. Almost every piece of music in the Renaissance featured polyphony. In addition, most vocal music in the Renaissance was *a cappella*.

Instruments in the Renaissance

As with the Middle Ages, earlier versions of the flute, recorder, violin, guitar, and various brass instruments existed, most of which were called by different names.

Performance Venues in the Renaissance

The church and the court continued to be important performance venues during the Renaissance.

Compositional and Performance Techniques of the Renaissance

Performance Technique: *A cappella* Singing

A cappella singing was popular in the Middle Ages and continued to be popular in the Renaissance.

Genres that feature *a cappella* singing:

- Mass
- Motets
- Madrigals

Compositional Technique: High Renaissance Style

The **High Renaissance style** was a style in which the textures used in any particular piece of music alternated between polyphony (mainly imitative) and homophony. It was as though the composers wanted to show off their abilities to write elaborate polyphony, yet also wanted to show that they could write a lush rich homophony. This style flourished from the middle of the Renaissance right through the end of the era. Almost every genre in the second half of the Renaissance used this style.

Compositional Technique: Paraphrase

Paraphrase was when a composer took a pre-existing melody and rewrote it to use within a new composition. They could change the rhythm, add extra notes—in some cases, a lot of extra notes—anything at all to make the melody sound more interesting than its original form. Because the main genres in the Middle Ages used a pre-existing plainchant as the basis for composition, it made sense for composers to continue doing that to some degree in the Renaissance. Paraphrase was used quite frequently in Masses. After selecting the pre-existing chant, they would then paraphrase it differently in each Ordinary section of the Mass. This created a sense of unity throughout the Mass. Even though plainchants were the main type of melody paraphrased, after a time, composers started paraphrasing secular tunes as well.

Genres that used paraphrase:

- Mass
- Motet

Compositional Technique: Word Painting

Word painting was a technique in which composers attempted to illustrate, through music, the words being sung. In other words, if the words of a song were "ascending into heav'n," the composer would set that text to an ascending note pattern. Here are some visual examples of word painting:

As you can see the "hopping" of the words is replicated/illustrated by the written notes. This example would be easily seen and easily heard.

This example may not be quite as easy to *hear* the word painting, but visually, the notes appear to take on the shape of a slithering snake.

Word painting continued to be popular in the next time period, although not quite as obviously.

Genres that used word painting: Any Renaissance vocal genres could use this technique, although it was most used in madrigals.

Genres of the Renaissance

Madrigal

A **madrigal** was a song in the High Renaissance Style (alternating sections of polyphony and homophony) for *a cappella* multiple voices. Madrigals could be either sacred or secular, but the vast majority were secular, with widely varying topics. Initially, madrigals flourished in Italy then spread to other European countries. Madrigals often featured word painting, sometimes to an extreme degree. Madrigals from England are particularly popular to this day.

Performing forces: *A cappella* singers.

Compositional techniques used in madrigals:

- High Renaissance style
- Word painting

FURTHER INVESTIGATION:

1. Listen to a number of madrigals to see if you can hear the word painting and the use of the High Renaissance style.
2. Look at the text of a madrigal before you listen to it, to see if you can determine which words will be "painted." Then listen to it to see if you were right.
3. Listen to an Italian madrigal without the text in front of you and try to guess which words are being painted simply by listening. Then look at a translation of the text to see if you were correct.

SUGGESTED LISTENING:

- Luca Marenzio's *Solo e pensoso i piu deserti campi*
- Carlo Gesualdo's *Moro, lasso, al mio duolo*
- Michael East's *Quick, quick, away, dispatch!*
- John Farmer's *Fair Phyllis I Saw Sitting All Alone* and *A Little Pretty Bonny Lass*

Motet

Motets in the Renaissance were quite different from the motets of the Middle Ages. Motets in the Renaissance were sacred *a cappella* vocal music in the High Renaissance style. In many ways they were almost exactly like madrigals except for the fact that they were sacred in nature and the text was in Latin.

Performing forces: *A cappella* voices.

Compositional techniques used in Renaissance motets:

- High Renaissance style
- Word painting

Exceptions to the definition above: There were such things as secular motets. But the vast majority were sacred.

SUGGESTED LISTENING:

- Jan Pieterszoon Sweelinck's *Hodie Christus natus est*
- Orlando de Lasso's *Quare tristis es anima mea?*
- William Byrd's *Domine, tu jurasti*

Mass

The structural and textual elements of the Mass in the Renaissance were the same as they were in the Middle Ages. The main difference was in the compositional techniques used. Plainchants and *a cappella* singing continued to be popular, but after the polyphonic genres in the Middle Ages evolved, such as organa, composers developed new styles of polyphonic and homophonic techniques, for example, the High Renaissance style.

In the Renaissance, there were a variety of Masses and compositional techniques used. Among these were

- **Missa brevis**—This means "short Mass." Each section of the Ordinary was much shorter than normal. Sometimes, the Gloria and the Credo (the two Ordinary sections that had the longest text) were left out entirely.

- **Paraphrase Mass**—A Mass in which a pre-existing melody was reworked by adding rhythm or extra notes to make it more interesting. Then, each section of the Ordinary used the same melody but paraphrased it slightly differently each time. This provided a musical unity to the Mass. Here is an example of a pre-existing plainchant (Ex. 1), followed by the paraphrased version for one of the Ordinary sections of the Mass (Ex. 2).

Ex. 1—plainchant

Ex. 2—paraphrase of plainchant

Here are both examples again, with lines drawn between to show exactly which notes have been used from the original to the paraphrase:

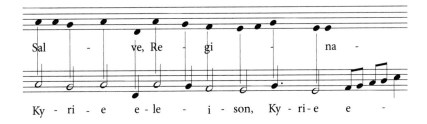

- **Parody Mass**, or Imitation Mass—A Mass in which each Ordinary portion of the Mass began with (or had a section with) the *exact* same notes in *all* voice parts as a pre-existing piece of music. For instance, the first example on the following page is an excerpt from a motet and the example immediately below it is an excerpt from a Mass, both of which use identical voicing.

Motet

Mass

<u>Performing forces:</u> *A cappella* singing. Near the end of the Renaissance, instruments became more common in church music.

<u>Compositional techniques used in the Mass in *this* time period:</u>

- Paraphrase
- Parody
- High Renaissance style

FURTHER INVESTIGATION:

1. Listen to a Mass composed in the Renaissance. Notice the texture of the different sections of the Mass to see if the Ordinary sections are more elaborate than the Proper sections. Note how it is different from a Mass composed in the Middle Ages. Listen for the High Renaissance style.
2. Listen to a paraphrase Mass but first listen to the composition that is being paraphrased so that you'll recognize the paraphrases when you hear them.

SUGGESTED LISTENING:

- Paraphrase Mass: Josquin's *Pange lingua Mass*. Listen to a recording of the *Pange lingua* plainchant to listen to first, so you can hear what was paraphrased.
- Parody Mass: Josquin's *Missa Malheur me bat*. Listen to Okeghem's chanson *Malheur me bat*, so you can try to hear what was imitated. (Note: This is a bit harder to hear than paraphrase, so you might also need to find a score of each piece to compare back and forth.)
- Missa brevis: Palestrina's *Missa brevis*.

Dance Music

There was a plethora of dance genres in the Renaissance. Some were formal, stately processional-style dances, while others were less formal folk dances. Here is a list of some of the dances in the Renaissance with a brief description regarding form and style.

- Allemande—moderate tempo, duple meter

- Basse danse—stately court dance, sometimes in duple meter, sometimes in triple
- Corrente—a fast dance in triple meter (Italy)
- Courante—a slow dance in triple meter (France)
- Galliard—lively with complex choreography, usually triple meter
- Jig—upbeat, jumping dance, triple (or compound duple) meter (England)
- Pavane—moderately slow processional dance, duple meter
- Saltarello—jumping dance, usually in triple meter (Italy)

The dance forms used in the Renaissance (for dancing) evolved into musical forms intended for listening. Look for the names of types of Renaissance dances to appear in Baroque suites and Classical chamber music.

Performing forces: Instruments in various combinations.

FURTHER INVESTIGATION:

1. Watch online videos of Renaissance dances to see how they looked and sounded.
2. Search for audio examples of a particular dance type. Most of the results you will find will be from the Renaissance and some will be from subsequent time periods. Listen to examples of both Renaissance AND later time periods to see how they follow a similar form.

SUGGESTED LISTENING:

- Allemande – Stefano Bernardi's "Allemande IV" from *Suite No. 3*
- Basse danse – Tylman Susato's *Danse du Roy*
- Corrente – Alessandro Piccinini's "Corrente III" from *Intavolatura di Liuto, et di Chitarrone, Book 1*
- Courante – Jakub Reys' *Courante*
- Galliard – Antony Holborne's *Galliard No. 2*
- Jig – John Dowland's *Tarleton's Jig*
- Pavane – Pierre Phalèse's *Pavane sur la bataille*
- Saltarello – Giorgio Mainerio's *Saltarello*

Composers of the Renaissance

Carlo Gesualdo (c. 1560–1613)

<u>Country:</u> Italy
<u>Interesting facts:</u>

- Nobleman—was both a prince and a count
- After he discovered his wife was having an affair, he had his servants help him kill both her and her lover. Because he was a nobleman, he was not prosecuted.

<u>Best known for:</u>

- Genre: Madrigals.
- Composition: *Moro, lasso al mio duolo*

<u>Highly recommended:</u> *Deh come in van sospiro*

Giovanni Pierluigi da Palestrina (c. 1525–1594)

<u>Country:</u> Italy
<u>Interesting facts:</u>

- Spent most of his life writing sacred music, including masses and motets. He did write some secular music, but later said that he "repented" of it.
- Is often credited for "saving church music" when the Catholic Church threatened to ban polyphony from the church because it feared it obscured the meaning of the words. The story goes (and it is most likely only a

story) that he composed a Mass in the High Renaissance style, but kept the imitative polyphony to a minimum. Then, when the church leaders heard it, he asked them if they understood all the words. They responded "yes" and he pointed out that it had polyphony in it, so they shouldn't ban it.

<u>Best known for:</u>

- Genre: Mass—he wrote over 100 of them.
- Composition: *Missa Papae Marcelli*

<u>Highly recommended:</u> *E, se 'l pensier*

Thomas Weelkes (1576–1623)

<u>Country:</u> England
<u>Interesting facts:</u>

- Works include both a considerable amount of church music and secular vocal music.

<u>Best known for:</u>

- Genre: Madrigals
- Composition: *As Vesta was from Latmos Hill Descending*

<u>Highly recommended:</u> *Ha ha! This world doth pass*

Other Composers

NAME	DATES	COUNTRY	GENRE
Binchois, Gilles	c. 1400–1460	Holland	Sacred and secular
Byrd, William	c. 1540–1623	England	Sacred and secular
Dufay, Guillaume	c. 1400–1470	Holland	Mass, Motet
Dunstable, John	c. 1390–1453	England	Mass, Motet
Farmer, John	c. 1570–c. 1600	England	Madrigals
Gabrieli, Giovanni	c. 1554–1612	Italy	Motet
Isaac, Heinrich	c. 1450–1517	Netherlands	Sacred and secular
Janequin, Clement	c. 1485–1558	France	Secular songs
Jeune, Claude le	c. 1530–1600	France	Secular
Josquin des Prez	c. 1450–1521	France	Mostly sacred
Lassus, Orlande de	c. 1532–1594	France	Sacred and secular
Marenzio, Luca	c. 1553–1599	Italy	Madrigals
Morales, Cristóbal de	c. 1500–1553	Spain	Sacred
Mouton, Jean	c. 1459–1522	France	Motets
Ockeghem, Johannes	c. 1410–1497	France	Sacred and secular
Tallis, Thomas	c. 1505–1585	England	Sacred
Taverner, John	c. 1490–1545	England	Sacred
Wert, Giaches de	1535–1596	Belgium	Secular
Willaert, Adrian	c. 1489–1562	Belgium	Sacred

BAROQUE ERA (1600-1750)

The Baroque Era was a time of great advancement in the amount of music written for orchestral instruments. In the previous time period—the Renaissance—most instrumental music was dance music or merely accompaniment for the human voice—the instruments were not the main focus. In the Baroque Era the focus shifted to instrumental music that was meant to be listened to.

Instruments in the Baroque Era

Most of the instruments with which we are familiar today became common in the Baroque Era. Baroque flutes, oboes, bassoons, and the most common brass instruments were simpler than their modern counterparts, but essentially sounded the same. Baroque string instruments were of an extremely high quality. In fact, string instruments built in the Baroque Era by the famous luthiers Antonio Stradivari and Andrea Guarneri are now worth millions of dollars because of the high quality of their construction. The most common keyboard instrument in the Baroque Era was the harpsichord, but by the mid-1700's, the piano was being perfected and gaining in popularity.

Performance Venues in the Baroque Era

The church and the court continued to be important performance venues in the Baroque Era. In addition, opera houses began to be built all over Europe. Operas were initially performed in theaters built by the nobility in their homes or on their estates. Only the wealthy and their invited guests were able to experience this new genre. As it became more popular, public opera houses offered tickets to the general public. Another important venue in the Baroque Era was the home. Members of the nobility, as well as the general public, performed chamber music in their homes as a form of domestic entertainment.

Compositional and Performance Techniques and Forms Used in the Baroque Era

Performance Technique: Basso Continuo

B**asso continuo** was a technique in which improvised chords were added to the bass line in a piece of music. The chords were improvised by a keyboard player (or guitar-type instrument). The keyboard player was provided with the same bass line as the lower instruments in the performing ensemble (usually cello and bass in an orchestra; cello or bassoon in a chamber ensemble); based on his training, the keyboardist would complete, or "realize," the bass line through improvisation.

This technique makes listening to Baroque music particularly interesting because you will never hear the same piece realized in exactly the same way. Every keyboard player is a unique individual with varied training and experience, so every keyboard player will realize the chords in a slightly different way. Note: any instrument that is assigned to play the bass line is referred to as a "continuo" player.

Genres that used basso continuo:

- All orchestral genres—concerto, orchestral suite, sinfonia.
- Most vocal genres—oratorio, cantata, Mass.
- Most chamber ensembles.

<u>Exceptions to the definition above:</u> In subsequent eras, keyboardists were no longer trained to improvise chords based solely on a bass line. As a result, music publishers began realizing the bass line for the keyboardists and publishing a separate keyboard part with the chords written out. Modern keyboardists are probably grateful for this.

FURTHER INVESTIGATION: Listen to three or four recordings of the same piece of music to see how different the keyboard improvisations can be. To ensure that the recordings are historically accurate, pick performing groups known for historical accuracy such as Tafelmusik, the Academy of Ancient Music, Concentus Musicus Wien, and the Aulos Ensemble.

Compositional Technique: Figured Bass

Figured bass is a set of symbols written above or below the bass line to help keyboardists realize the bass line. Here's what it looks like on the printed page:

There was still plenty of freedom for the keyboardist to improvise even within the suggested chords provided by the figured bass.

<u>Genres that used figured bass:</u> Any compositions that feature basso continuo can also feature figured bass.

Compositional Technique: Walking Bass

Walking bass was a technique in which every note in the bass line was the same length. Walking bass could be featured throughout an entire piece or it could be used for sections within a piece. The visual examples below show a variety of walking bass lines.

Example 1:

Example 2:

Example 3:

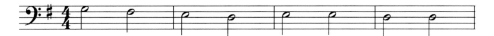

Genres that used walking bass: Composers could use this technique in any genre.

SUGGESTED LISTENING:

- Johann Sebastian Bach's "Wiewohl mein Herz in Tränen schwimmt" from *St. Matthew Passion, BWV 244*
- Bach's "Erbarme dich, mein Gott" from *St Matthew Passion, BWV 244*

Compositional Technique: Ground Bass

Ground bass was a bass line in which the succession of pitches (the melody of the bass line) repeat over and over again. Ground bass could be featured throughout an entire piece or it could be used for sections within a piece. The visual examples below show a variety of ground bass lines. You can easily see the repetition of each ground bass pattern.

Example 1:

Example 2:

Example 3:

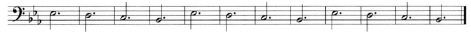

Note that the third example of ground bass is also a walking bass!

<u>Genres that used ground bass:</u> Composers could use ground bass technique in any genre.

SUGGESTED LISTENING:

- Johann Pachelbel's *Canon in D major* (This is undoubtedly the most famous ground bass of all time.)
- Henry Purcell's "When I Am Laid in Earth" from *Dido and Aeneas*.
- Claudio Monteverdi's "Pur ti miro" from Act III of *L'incoronazione di Poppea*.

Form: Fugue

The **fugue** was one of the most popular forms in the Baroque Era. It was highly structured and featured almost non-stop imitative polyphony.

The first section of a fugue was called an **exposition**. The exposition began with the main melody being sounded by a single "voice." ("Voice" means either the human voice or an instrumental voice. Most fugues in the Baroque Era were instrumental.) The main melody, stated by "Voice One" was called the **subject**. The subject is represented in this diagram by a jagged line.

subject

Voice 1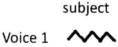

As soon as Voice One was finished stating the subject, Voice Two imitated Voice One by restating the subject. The composer could choose to have Voice Two state the subject at exactly the same pitches as Voice One OR higher or lower than Voice One. But regardless of how high or how low Voice Two was, the subject would be recognizable as the same subject with which Voice One began the fugue.

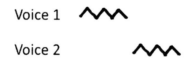

While Voice Two stated the subject, Voice One continued with new musical material that sounded good with Voice Two. This new musical material is represented here by the looped line.

Voice 1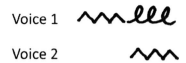

Voice 2

Composers could use as many voices as they wanted in a fugue. The majority of fugues had three or four voices, but they could have as few as two, or as many as the composer's skill and imagination could handle.

Any additional voices in a fugue would also take their turns stating the subject. Therefore, if it was a three-voice fugue, after Voice Two stated the subject, Voice Three would state the subject. If it was a four-voice fugue, after Voice Three stated the subject, Voice Four would state the subject. And again, composers could use as many voices as they felt they could maintain.

Even though this was a fairly rigid form, the composer still had opportunities to make creative choices. For instance, when each new voice entered, the composer could have the previous voice state the same new musical material Voice One stated when Voice Two began the subject, as this diagram shows:

Voice 1

Voice 2

Voice 3

Voice 4

OR, composers could have each new voice introduce completely new musical material when the subsequent voices were stating the subject, as this diagram shows:

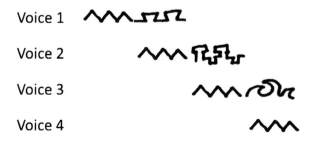

Voice 1

Voice 2

Voice 3

Voice 4

In addition, the composer could choose to have all voices continue with new musical material, like so:

It was also possible for the composer to have one of the voices drop out for a time.

Another option for the composer was to insert a **bridge** between voices two and three, or between voices three and four, or between voices four and five, etc., like so:

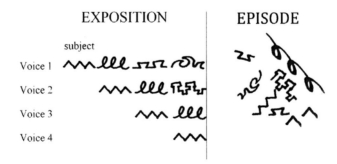

A bridge was extra musical material to stretch the piece out a little bit. The only place a bridge could not happen was between voices one and two, because if voice two hadn't entered yet, we would assume it was just a really long subject.

When the last voice in a particular fugue finished stating the subject, the exposition was over and the next part began. The next part was called the **episode**. In an episode, the composer reworked the material that had already been presented in the exposition.

To illustrate the types of things a composer could do to rework the material from the exposition (for use in the episode), here is a subject:

Composers used what were called **fugal devices** to create new musical material (for the episode) from the material that already existed (in the exposition). The most commonly used fugal devices were

1) **retrograde**, or, in other words, backwards.

2) **inversion**—played upside down:

3) **retrograde inversion**—upside down and backwards:

4) **diminution**—making the note values shorter:

5) **augmentation**—making the note values longer:

6) **fragmentation**—chopping the musical material up and only using pieces of it.

The principles of all these fugal devices could also be applied to each other, for instance, a retrograde augmented fragment or an inverted diminution. After the episode, at some point, the subject returned in its entirety (it may have been fragmented in the episode). After it returned, there would be another episode. Then another subject return, another episode, another subject return, and so on, as illustrated here:

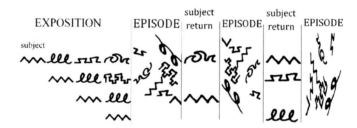

Fugues usually ended with a final clear statement of the subject.

Here is the complete exposition of a four-voice fugue—"Contrapunctus I" from *Kunst der Fuge*—by Bach (in his own handwriting), with each voice labeled.

As you can see, there is no bridge in this exposition—just one voice stating the subject after another. Here is "Fugue #5 in D Major" from the *Well-Tempered Klavier* by Bach:

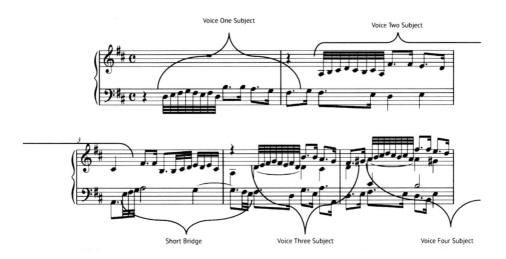

As you can see, in this four-voice fugue, there is a short bridge between voices two and three.

<u>Genres that used fugue form:</u> Any. You can find full fugues paired with other pieces of music—for example *Toccata and Fugue*, *Fantasia and Fugue*, or *Prelude and Fugue*. You can also find fugal sections within a piece of music.

FURTHER INVESTIGATION:

1. Listen to a number of fugues. Try to determine how many voices are in each fugue and whether bridges are used or not.
2. Do a search for "fugue" and "pop music" or "Broadway" or "modern" to see how the fugue continues to be influential.

SUGGESTED LISTENING:

- Johann Sebastian Bach's "Fugue #10 in E minor" from the *Well-Tempered Klavier*—it is a two-voice fugue and the subject is quite short.
- Bach's "Fugue #6 in D minor" from the *Well-Tempered Klavier*—three-voice fugue, no bridge.
- Bach's *"Little" Organ Fugue in G Minor, S. 578*—four voices with a really short bridge between voices two and three.

- Bach's "Fugue #22 in F minor" from the *Well-Tempered Klavier*—five voices with a long bridge between voices two and three, and a short bridge between voices four and five.

Form: Ritornello

A piece in **ritornello** form began with musical material played by a large group of instruments, usually an orchestra. This initial musical material was called the "ritornello" or, in other words, "this music will return again." Following the first statement of the ritornello, there was a solo section featuring one soloist (or a small group of soloists) supported by the continuo players. Next there was a return to the musical material first heard in the ritornello. Composers didn't have to repeat the entire ritornello; they could use a fragment of it, as long as the listeners could recognize it as material from the opening section. The remainder of the piece proceeded back and forth between solo sections and ritornello sections for as long as the composer wanted to keep the piece going.

There were many possibilities of how to diagram ritornello form, since the composers could go back and forth as long as they wanted, but the easiest diagram is as follows:

Ritornello/Solo 1/Ritorn./Solo 2/Ritorn./Solo 3/Ritorn./Solo 4/Ritorn./Solo 5/etc.

Genres that used ritornello form:

- Concerto and concerto grosso, usually in the first movement and sometimes in the third movement as well.
- Opera.
- Trio sonata, and other chamber music.

FURTHER INVESTIGATION:

1. Listen to any first movement of a concerto from the Baroque Era. Determine whether or not it follows ritornello form (approximately 90% of the time it will).
2. Go onto a music-streaming website and search the word "ritornello." Try to find as many different genres that feature ritornello form as possible.

SUGGESTED LISTENING:

- Concerto/Concerto Grosso—Johann Sebastian Bach's *Brandenburg Concerto #5 in D, BWV 1050*, first movement.
- Opera—Claudio Monteverdi's "Dal mio Permesso amato" from *L'Orfeo*

- Cantata—Adam Krieger's *An den Wassern zu Babel*

<u>Exceptions to the definition above:</u> Before ritornello form (as diagrammed above) became popular, the word "ritornello" was used to label ANY section of instrumental music that provided a break between numbers in a vocal/choral work, such as opera, oratorio, or cantata. Don't be surprised if you do a search for ritornello and find a random number in an opera that is only 45 seconds long. The "return" in that case was usually that the ritornello had similar melodic or harmonic elements as the vocal piece that preceded it.

Form: French Overture

An overture was generally a piece of music that began a multi-movement com-position or an entertainment like an opera or oratorio. One of the most popular forms for composing an overture in the Baroque Era was what is known as **French overture**. A French overture had two sections:

1. A slow opening section with dotted rhythms (a long note followed by a short note—long-short-long-short-long-short)
2. A faster section featuring imitative polyphony, quite often a fugue.

<u>Genres that used French overture form:</u>

- Suite
- Opera
- Oratorio

FURTHER INVESTIGATION: Listen to a number of Baroque opera overtures. Try to determine which are "French."

SUGGESTED LISTENING:

- George Frideric Handel's overture to *Water Music Suite in F, HWV 348*
- Henry Purcell's overture to *Dido and Aeneas*
- Handel's overture to *Messiah*

Form: *Da Capo* Aria

A *da capo* **aria** was a song in three sections—ABA. The singer sang the first A section then the contrasting B section. The words *da capo* would be printed in the music at the end of the B section. *Da capo* means "to the top" so the singer would go back to the beginning and sing the A section again. However, this time the singer would improvise extra notes, ornaments, and flashy scales to make it more interesting.

Genres that used *da capo* arias:

- Opera
- Oratorio
- Cantata

FURTHER INVESTIGATION: Look at the music for a *da capo* aria to see the indication for *da capo* (or D.C.) at the end of the B section.

SUGGESTED LISTENING:

- George Frideric Handel's "Iris, Hence Away!" from *Semele, HWV 58*
- Handel's "Rejoice Greatly" from *Messiah, HWV 56*
- Johann Sebastian Bach's "Jauchzet Gott in allen Landen!" from *Jauchzet Gott in allen Landen!, BWV 51*

Performing Technique: Castrati

Castrati were men who were castrated before puberty in order to prevent their voices from dropping in pitch. Castrati were very popular in Baroque opera initially playing female roles (since the Catholic Church looked down on women performing in theatrical productions) but, due to their popularity, eventually taking on the male lead roles. A castrato sounds almost exactly like a female soprano.

By the end of the Baroque Era, the general public no longer approved of the procedure required to create castrati. The popularity of the castrati died out quite quickly. Nowadays, when an opera company wants to produce a Baroque opera that requires a castrato, they use a countertenor instead.

Genres that used castrati:

- Opera seria
- Oratorio

SUGGESTED LISTENING:

- Recordings featuring modern-day countertenors David Daniels or Lawrence Zazzo.
- Historical recordings of Alessandro Moreschi, a castrato who lived *just* long enough to see the advent of recording technology.

Genres of the Baroque Era

Concerto/Concerto Grosso

A **concerto** (plural: concerti) was an instrumental genre featuring one solo instrument and a Baroque orchestra. The focus was on the interplay between the solo instrument and the orchestra; each vied for our attention in different ways.

A **concerto grosso** was a concerto that had more than one soloist. In the early Baroque, composers wrote concerti grossi for a small group of soloists, called the **concertino**, and a group of accompanying instruments, called the **ripieno**. The ripieno could be a small group of instruments or even a full Baroque orchestra.

In both types of concerto (solo or grosso) there were usually three movements. Generally, the first movement was fast; second was slow; and third was fast.

Sometimes composers indicated genre (in this case, concerto grosso) in the title and other times they specified the individual instruments that were the soloists. If you see a concerto title that indicates multiple soloists, you can be certain that it is a concerto grosso.

Initially, concerti had many movements, but eventually the three movement structure mentioned above became standard. The genre of concerto continued to be popular in subsequent time periods all the way up to and including the present day. The concerto grosso was most popular in the Baroque Era, but examples of concerti grossi showed up in each of the subsequent time periods, but with much less frequency than the solo concerto (which has remained popular with composers and performers up to the present day).

<u>Forms/techniques used in concerti:</u>

- Ritornello form (usually used in the first movement; sometimes in the third).
- **Cadenza**—a cadenza was a moment during the concerto in which the orchestra arrived at a cadence chord and stopped playing while the soloist improvised an unaccompanied solo for as long as the soloist deemed appropriate.

FURTHER INVESTIGATION:

1. Listen to a shuffled playlist of concerti and concerti grossi. Try to determine whether each piece is a solo concerto or a concerto grosso.
2. Listen to determine whether ritornello form is being used or not.

SUGGESTED LISTENING:

- Johann Sebastian Bach's *Brandenburg Concerto #4 in G, BWV 1049*
- Antonio Vivaldi's *Concerto for Mandolin and Strings in C Major, RV 425*
- Georg Philipp Telemann's *Trumpet Concerto in D, TWV 51/D7*

<u>Exceptions to the definitions above:</u> At an instrumental recital, if a concerto is listed, the assumption would be that the performance would feature a solo performer with orchestral accompaniment. However, most solo performers, aren't going to go to the effort and expense of hiring a full orchestra for their recital. In these cases, they use what is called a **piano reduction**, or, in other words, a piano arrangement of the orchestral score.

Suite

A **suite** was a multi-movement work in which the first movement was an introduction of sorts (an overture or prelude, for example) and subsequent movements were based on dances. However, suites were not intended for dancing; they were meant for listening pleasure. All the movements in a suite were in the same key. There was no standard number of movements in this genre—it varied widely.

The genre of the suite was quite versatile; a suite could be composed for a solo instrument, a small group of instruments, or even a full Baroque orchestra. If for a solo instrument, or small group of instruments, the suite was a chamber genre, intended for performance in the home. If for orchestra, the suite was intended for performance in a concert setting.

The suite fell out of favor after the Baroque Era for quite some time, but then in the Romantic Era, composers began grouping pieces of instrumental music from various genres together and titled this new grouping a "suite." For instance, Georges Bizet wrote the opera *Carmen* and then later selected certain sections of the opera, rewrote them for orchestra (no voice), and grouped them together in a multi-movement suite titled *Carmen Suite*. Tchaikovsky wrote the ballet *Sleeping Beauty* and later selected certain sections from the ballet and grouped them together as *Sleeping Beauty Suite*. In the 20th century, composers created orchestral suites based on a series of related topics, for instance, Gustav Holst's famous suite, *The Planets*, in which each movement is representative of a different planet. In these later suites, the movements were no longer unified by key. In fact, these later suites bear almost no similarity to the suites of the Baroque Era except for the fact that they all have multiple movements.

FURTHER INVESTIGATION: Listen to a movement of a suite that shares a name with a Renaissance dance form (for instance, "allemande" or "courante"), then listen to the Renaissance equivalent to see the evolution from Renaissance to Baroque.

SUGGESTED LISTENING:

- Solo instrument suite—Johann Sebastian Bach's *Cello Suite No. 3 in C major, BWV 1009*
- Keyboard suite—Dietrich Buxtehude's *Suite in D minor, BuxWV 233, "D'amour"*
- Chamber ensemble suite—Marin Marais' "Suite in A minor" from *Pieces de viole, Book 3*
- Orchestral suite—George Frideric Handel's *Music for the Royal Fireworks, HWV 351*

Sonata

Defining the word **sonata** is quite tricky for a variety of reasons. The word itself translates (from the Italian) as "sounded." The term was used initially to set instrumental music apart from vocal music ("cantata") and keyboard music ("toccata," meaning "touched.") In other words, ALL purely instrumental music could be referred to as "sonata." The genre of sonata was a domestic genre, meaning that sonatas were intended to be played in the home. (This also meant that sonatas belonged to the larger genre of chamber music.) Most sonatas in the Baroque Era were either solo sonatas for one instrument or duo sonatas for one orchestral instrument plus a keyboard instrument (or, in some cases, continuo).

There was no set number of movements in the Baroque Era sonata, although the most common number was four movements (slow-fast-slow-fast). Three- and five-movement sonatas were also quite common.

SUGGESTED LISTENING:

- Antonio Vivaldi's *Flute Sonata No. 6 in G minor, Op. 13, RV 58, "Il pastor fido"*
- Johann Sebastian Bach's *Violin Sonata No. 1 in G minor, BWV 1001*

Trio Sonata

The **trio sonata** was a type of chamber music, intended to be performed in the home. One might assume that a trio sonata was performed by three musicians, but that was not the case—trio sonatas actually needed more than three players; two higher instruments, such as the violin or flute, and one "basso continuo" part. Trio sonatas required, at the very least, four performers.

Because this developed as a domestic genre—meaning it was performed in the comfort of one's home by amateur musicians—a lot of the time, the composer wouldn't specify which instruments were to be used. It all depended on which instruments your family or friends played.

The trio sonata had no specified number of movements, but the most common was a four-movement structure, generally beginning with a slow movement.

SUGGESTED LISTENING:

- Jean-Baptiste Loeillet's *Trio Sonata in F major, Op. 2, No. 2*
- Georg Philipp Telemann's *Trio Sonata in C minor, TWV 42:c2*
- George Frideric Handel's *Trio Sonata in G minor, Op. 2, No. 2, HWV 387*

Exceptions to the definition above: Some composers occasionally combined all three parts of the trio sonata into one keyboard piece, so the title appeared even more confusing because the word "trio" was in the title, yet only one instrument performed it.

Opera

Opera was a genre in which a story was told through singing and acting, complete with sets and costumes. This genre, developed in the latter half of the Renaissance, became very popular among the nobility in the first thirty years of the Baroque Era, and then became available to the general public as opera houses were built all over Europe starting in 1637. Most operas in the early Baroque were quite short, often less than an hour, but by the middle of the Baroque Era, operas could last anywhere from an hour to over three hours. To compose an opera, a composer would start by obtaining a **libretto** from a librettist. A libretto—literally "little book"—was the text of the opera. Some composers worked with the same librettist for years on multiple operas; other times, they'd work with different librettists for each opera.

There were two basic types of opera in the Baroque Era—**opera seria** and **opera buffa**.

Opera seria was "serious" opera. The storylines were highly influenced by mythology and/or history, usually telling stories of the triumphs of historical military leaders or royalty. This appealed to members of the nobility of the Baroque Era because they often liked to compare themselves to triumphant leaders of the past. In many cases, court composers wrote operas quite overt in the glorification of their employer. The heroes in these operas were sung by the higher voice types—soprano, tenor, and castrato—because the audiences of the day preferred the higher voice to the lower voice.

Opera buffa, on the other hand, was comic opera, and was more popular in the public opera houses. The storylines were generally about a servant triumphing over an employer in some way. Members of nobility were usually depicted as buffoons and sung by the lower voice types—bass and alto. Servants were depicted as wise and kind and were sung by the higher voice types—soprano, tenor, and castrato.

Within any opera, there were different kinds of musical numbers. These were called recitative, aria, ensemble, and chorus.

Recitative

A **recitative** was a section within an opera in which narration was sung by a solo singer or dialogue was sung between multiple singers. There were two basic types of recitative—secco and accompanied. "Secco" means "dry." Therefore secco recitative was fairly speech-like (a descendant of recitation) and accompanied by fairly sparse chords from the continuo players. Accompanied recitative, on the other hand, had much more accompaniment from the continuo players and/or orchestra.

Aria

An **aria** was a section within an opera in which a solo singer reflected on a particular plot point, usually focusing on his/her emotions. Arias were highly melodic, highly repetitive, and had solid homophonic accompaniment from the continuo players and/or orchestra. Arias could be composed in a number of forms, but *da capo* form was the most popular. Arias could also feature cadenzas.

Ensemble

An **ensemble** (in opera) was any aria-like section in which there was more than one singer—mainly duos and trios.

Chorus

A **chorus** was a musical number for a larger group of singers.
Performing forces: Vocal soloists, chorus, and orchestra.

Forms used in opera:

- Da capo aria
- French overture

SUGGESTED LISTENING:

- Marc-Antoine Charpentier's *La Descente d'Orphée aux Enfers, H. 488*
- George Frideric Handel's *Giulio Cesare in Egitto, HWV 17*
- Henry Purcell's *Dido and Aeneas*

Exceptions to the definitions above: At a vocal recital, if an aria from an opera is listed, the assumption would be that the performance would feature a solo singer with orchestral accompaniment. However, most singers, when doing only one number from an opera, aren't going to go to the effort and expense of hiring a full orchestra for their recital. Instead, they would use a piano reduction of the orchestral score.

Oratorio

The genre of **oratorio** was very similar to opera due to the use of recitatives, arias, and choruses, and the fact that it told a dramatic story. Oratorio was different from opera in that it told a sacred story and it did not use sets or costumes. Although the genre originated in the church, it was often performed as part of a concert series, or in opera houses, for paying audiences.

Because oratorios were often performed in secular concert halls or opera houses, some composers wrote oratorios based on secular themes, for instance, Haydn's *The Seasons*.

Performing forces: Vocal soloists, chorus, and orchestra.

FURTHER INVESTIGATION: Handel's most famous work, *Messiah*, is perhaps the most-heard oratorio in history. It is extremely popular, especially around Christmastime when professional orchestras and choirs offer *Messiah* "sing-alongs" where the audience gets to join in on every chorus. Amateur productions also abound using a piano reduction or an orchestra made up of whatever instruments the local congregation boasts among its membership. Do a quick Internet search of "Messiah sing-along" and see what it yields.

SUGGESTED LISTENING:

- Scarlatti's *Agar et Ismaele Esiliati*
- Handel's *Israel in Egypt*
- Schutz's *Historia der frolichen und siegreichen Aufferstehung unsers einigen Erlosers und Seligmachers Jesu Christi* (also known as the "Christmas Oratorio")

Chorale

A **chorale** was the same thing as a hymn, similar to those sung in most Christian churches today—four-part harmony and very homophonic. Chorales originated in the Lutheran church and were in the German language. If a particular chorale was popular, numerous composers would take the chorale tune (main melody) and write new harmonizations/arrangements of the same chorale for use in their own compositions. This would be considered plagiarism today, but back then, it was considered a compliment if a chorale tune was "borrowed" by other composers.

Chorales pretty much always sound like a typical hymn. Though they originated in the Lutheran church, over the years other religions borrowed chorales from the Lutheran hymnal, wrote new texts and new harmonizations, and incorporated them into their own hymnals.

Performing forces: SATB (soprano, alto, tenor, bass), choir with keyboard, chamber, or orchestral accompaniment/support.

FURTHER INVESTIGATION: Look at the hymnal in your church to see if you can find a hymn attributed to Bach or Martin Luther (both Lutherans). Go to a different Christian church and look in their hymnal to see if you can find the same chorale tunes used.

SUGGESTED LISTENING:

- Johann Sebastian Bach's *Nun danket alle Gott (Now Thank We All Our God)* and *Wie soll ich dich empfangen (How Shall I Receive Thee)*

- *Ein feste Burg ist unser Gott (A Mighty Fortress Is Our God)* — very popular chorale tune attributed to Martin Luther and set (arranged) by numerous composers

Chorale Prelude

A **chorale prelude** was an arrangement of a chorale for solo organ. Despite the fact that the word "chorale" was in the genre title, no singing was involved. Chorale preludes were intended to introduce the hymn tune to the congregation before they sang the chorale as part of the church service.
Performing force: Organ.

FURTHER INVESTIGATION: Find some Lutheran chorales that you like. See if there is a chorale prelude version of that same chorale and listen to it.

SUGGESTED LISTENING:

- Johann Sebastian Bach's *Nun danket Alle Gott, BWV 657*
- Bach's *Wachet auf, ruft uns die Stimme, BWV 645*
- Bach's *Herzlich tut mich verlangen, BWV 727*

Cantata

A **cantata** was a relatively short, sacred, dramatic musical presentation (similar to oratorio) that was performed in the Lutheran church service. Because it had to fit within the confines of a typical Lutheran church service, the length of a cantata was usually between 15 and 30 minutes. Cantatas, like oratorios, featured recitatives, arias, and choruses, and did not use sets, acting, or costumes. The choruses used in a cantata were chorales, performed as a simple hymn, or, often elaborated upon with lots of orchestral interludes.

As mentioned earlier in the chapter, the word "cantata" means "a piece of music that is sung," which means that before the Lutheran church cantata, there were lots of other types of cantatas. After the Baroque Era, other religions borrowed the genre and you can find cantatas written by many composers in many religions.
Performing forces: Vocal soloists, choir, organ, continuo, orchestra.

SUGGESTED LISTENING:

- Johann Sebastian Bach's *Ein feste Burg ist unser Gott, BWV 80*
- Bach's *Lobe den Herren, den mächtigen König der Ehren, BWV 137*
- Bach's *Herz und Mund und Tat und Leben, BWV 147*

Mass

The Mass as a genre was still alive and well in the Baroque Era. It was used in both the Catholic and Lutheran churches, and the only real difference was that the musical style changed from the High Renaissance style to a much more Baroque style.

SUGGESTED LISTENING:

- Johann Sebastian Bach's *Mass in B minor, BWV 232*
- Johann David Heinichen's *Mass No. 11 in D major*
- Johann Ernst Eberlin's *Mass No. 34 in C major*

Composers of the Baroque Era

Tomaso Albinoni (1671–c. 1750)

<u>Country:</u> Italy
<u>Interesting facts:</u>

- Freelance composer—never a court or church composer.
- Extremely prolific—over 70 operas, 40 cantatas, 100 sonatas, 50 concerti.
- Best known for a piece of music he didn't even compose. For a good portion of the twentieth century, the listening public was entranced by *Adagio in G minor*, purportedly discovered by musicologist Remo Giazotto shortly after World War II. After much scholarly research, the majority opinion is that the piece was entirely composed by Giazotto and has no connection to Albinoni.

<u>Aside from the aforementioned *Adagio*, Albinoni is best known for:</u>

- Genre: Concerti and Sonatas
- Composition: *Oboe Concerto in D minor, Op. 9, No. 2* especially the 2nd movement.

<u>Highly recommended:</u> *Concerto a 5 in G minor, Op. 10, No. 2*

Johann Sebastian Bach (1685–1750)

Country: Germany
Interesting facts:

- Spent most of his life working in the Lutheran church.
- Wrote some of the best-known secular keyboard music in the world, notably *The Well-Tempered Klavier*.
- Not famous as a composer in his lifetime. Almost 80 years after his death, Romantic Era-composer Felix Mendelssohn produced a performance of Bach's *St. Matthew Passion*, which began a Bach revival. Bach has become continually more famous with each passing year.
- Went blind in the last ten years of life.

Best known for:

- Genre: Lutheran cantatas and Masses; secular keyboard and orchestral music
- Composition: *St. Matthew Passion*; *Brandenburg Concerti*

Highly recommended: *Was mir behagt, ist nur die muntre Jagd, BWV 208*, "Hunt Cantata," especially the fourth aria, "Schafe konnen sicher weiden."

Marc-Antoine Charpentier (1643–1704)

Country: France
Interesting facts:

- Spent most of his career working as the court composer for a wealthy noblewoman in Paris. At the same time he worked for several Jesuit churches. As a result, the majority of his works are sacred in nature.

Best known for:

- Genre: Sacred music
- Composition: *Te Deum, H. 146*

Highly recommended: *La Descente d'Orphée aux Enfers H. 488*, particularly "Je ne refuse point le secours" from Act II, scene 2.

George Frideric Handel (1685–1759)

<u>Country</u>: Germany
<u>Interesting facts:</u>

- Spent most of his life working in the secular world, particularly in the genres of opera seria and oratorio.
- During a duel, the opponent's sword broke when it hit Handel's coat button.

<u>Best known for:</u>

- Genre: Oratorios
- Composition: *Messiah*

<u>Highly recommended</u>: *Israel in Egypt*, particularly "He led them forth like sheep."

Jean-Baptiste Lully (1632–1687)

<u>Country</u>: Born in Italy; most of life spent in France
<u>Interesting facts:</u>

- Worked as a court composer for King Louis XIV of France.
- Wrote a number of ballets in which Louis XIV was the lead dancer.
- Unusual death. Lully was conducting a performance of one of his sacred works using his cane to keep time. He accidentally brought the staff down on one of his feet, stabbing it; it subsequently developed gangrene, and he died from the infection.

<u>Best known for:</u>

- Genre: Opera
- Composition: *Armide*

<u>Highly recommended</u>: "Air pour les Mesmes" from *Le mariage forcé Suite*

Henry Purcell (c. 1660–1695)

<u>Country:</u> England
<u>Interesting facts:</u>

- Spent most of his career as an organist at Westminster Abbey and is actually buried near the organ.
- Court composer for English royalty
- Composed secular songs, sacred music, instrumental suites, and opera.

<u>Best known for:</u>

- Genre: Opera
- Composition: *Dido and Aeneas*

<u>Highly recommended:</u> *A New Ground in E minor, Z. T682*

Antonio Vivaldi (1678–1741)

<u>Country:</u> Italy
<u>Interesting facts:</u>

- Most of his career was spent at the Ospedale della Pietà, an orphanage/school for girls. He was able to experiment and create his music with a built-in set of musicians ready to play for him.
- Wrote over forty operas, yet they are rarely performed today. His orchestral compositions are so popular they overshadow his operas.

<u>Best known for:</u>

- Genre: Concerti
- Composition: *The Four Seasons*

<u>Highly recommended:</u> *Concerto in A Minor for 2 Oboes & Strings, RV 536*

Other Composers

NAME	DATES	COUNTRY	GENRE
Aubert, Jacques	1689–1753	France	Sonata, Concerto, Opera
Bach, Carl Philipp Emanuel	1714–1788	Germany	Keyboard music
Bach, Wilhelm Friedemann	1710–1784	Germany	Keyboard music
Biber, Heinrich I. F. von	1644–1704	Germany	Violin sonata
Boismortier, Joseph B. de	1689–1755	France	Flute and Vocal music
Buxtehude, Dietrich	c. 1637–1707	Denmark	Cantata, Organ music
Corelli, Arcangelo	1653–1713	Italy	Sonata, Concerto
Couperin, François	1668–1733	France	Keyboard
Fasch, Johann Friedrich	1688–1758	Germany	Instrumental, Vocal
Fux, Johann Joseph	1660–1741	Austria	Opera, Oratorio, Mass
Graupner, Christoph	1683–1760	Germany	Sacred and secular
Guerre, Élisabeth J. de la	1665–1729	France	Keyboard, Sonata
Hasse, Johann Adolph	1699–1783	Germany	Opera seria
Hotteterre, Jacques-Martin	1674–1763	France	Flute music
Legrenzi, Giovanni	1626–1690	Italy	Sacred and secular
Locatelli, Pietro	1695–1764	Italy	Violin music
Loeillet, Jacques	1685–1748	Belgium	Oboe, Flute music
Loeillet, Jean-Baptiste	1688–1720	Belgium	Recorder music
Marais, Marin	1656–1728	France	Opera, Chamber music
Marcello, Benedetto	1686–1739	Italy	Cantata
Molter, Johann-Melchior	1696–1765	Germany	Instrumental music
Pachelbel, Johann	1653–1706	Germany	Organ, Chamber music
Pergolesi, Giovanni Battista	1710–1736	Italy	Opera buffa
Quantz, Johann Joachim	1697–1773	Germany	Flute music
Rameau, Jean-Philippe	1683–1764	France	Opera seria
Sammartini, Giuseppe	1695–1750	Italy	Instrumental music
Scarlatti, Domenico	1685–1757	Italy	Keyboard music
Strozzi, Barbara	1619–1677	Italy	Cantata, Vocal music
Tartini, Giuseppe	1692–1770	Italy	Violin music
Telemann, Georg Philipp	1681–1767	Germany	Opera, Chamber music
Torelli, Giuseppe	1658–1709	Italy	Instrumental music

Section 5

CLASSICAL ERA (1750–1830)

The music of the Classical Era focused on entertainment. Composers wanted audiences to leave at the end of a concert humming the tunes they had heard. Because of this, there was a definite shift toward homophonic music because it allowed the main melody to be the focal point. Polyphony was still used in the Classical Era, but less so than in the previous era.

Instruments in the Classical Era

Woodwind, brass, string, and keyboard instruments continued to be used and perfected during the Classical Era. In addition to the flute, oboe, and bassoon, the clarinet became a part of the orchestra. The most common keyboard instrument in the Baroque Era was the piano. The harpsichord was no longer an essential part of the orchestra (neither was the piano), but continued to be used, mainly in secco recitative sections in operas.

Performance Venues in the Classical Era

The church, court, opera house, and private home continued to be important performance venues in the Classical Era. In addition, concert halls began to become more common to showcase the rising genre of the symphony, and to make orchestral music more accessible to the general public.

Forms Used in the Classical Era

Many composers in the Classical Era felt the pressure of working for demanding patrons who expected new compositions almost on a daily basis. To alleviate this stress, composers relied on tried-and-true compositional forms to help them compose music with greater ease.

Form: Sonata

Sonata form was the most popular form in the Classical Era. It influenced composers in subsequent time periods including the present day. If listeners understand this form, even at its most basic, their enjoyment of music will increase; literally hundreds of compositions from this time period employed sonata form.

Sonata form can be diagrammed with a large ABA structure. The first A section was called the **exposition**. The B section was called the **development**. And the final A section was called the **recapitulation** and might be labeled with a prime, because, even though it was a repeat of the first A section, there were some pretty substantial changes as well.

The exposition "exposes" all the musical material that will be used for the remainder of the composition. Here is the order in which things occurred in the exposition:

1. **1st theme**—Usually a fairly simple melody with homophonic support in the tonic key. Occasionally, composers made the 1st theme a little more elaborate but usually it was quite hummable.
2. **Bridge**—A bridge could be of any length and it could be quite melodic or merely functional. Its purpose was to transition the composition from the tonic key to a closely related key (like the dominant). This closely related key could be higher or lower than the tonic key—whatever the composer wanted.
3. **2nd theme**—Another fairly simple melody in the new key.
4. **Cadence theme**—Yet another fairly simple melody, also in the new key, but this one ended with a solid cadence chord. A listener might be convinced that that was the end of the piece—that's how conclusive the cadence chord at the end of the cadence theme could sound. But it was not the end of the piece; it was only the end of the exposition.

The development featured the musical material from the exposition but the composer reworked, or "developed" it. There wasn't a set pattern for the development—composers could fragment motives from the exposition, draw them out, elaborate upon them, etc. (This may remind you of the episode in a fugue.) The only thing all developments had in common was modulation. At the end of the development, there was a feeling of suspense; the music sounded like it was heading somewhere. This moment was called the **retransition**. Its purpose was to prepare for the return of the tonic. Earlier, the bridge functioned as a transition from the tonic key to a new key. The retransition took the piece back to the tonic key and to the third section of sonata form.

The recapitulation began with the 1st theme from the exposition because, as previously mentioned, the recapitulation was a repeat of the exposition—1st theme, bridge, 2nd theme, and cadence theme all occurred again. The difference this time was that it all stayed in the tonic key. The bridge no longer served its original function. Because the original purpose of the bridge was to modulate from one key to another, the composer had to rework the way the bridge sounded; the composer may have had to quickly modulate through a few keys to force the bridge to end up back in the tonic key so that the remainder of the recapitulation could stay in the tonic key.

Here's what it looked like all put together:

A	Exposition	1st theme • Hummable melody • In the tonic key Bridge • Modulates the piece to a new key • Can be short or long 2nd theme • New hummable melody • In the new key Cadence theme • New hummable melody • Stays in the new key • Ends with a final-sounding cadence
B	Development	Reworking earlier material • Lots of modulation • Usually quite polyphonic Retransition • Sounds like it is leading to something important • Takes the piece back to tonic key
A	Recapitulation	1st theme • In the tonic key Bridge • Remains in the tonic key 2nd theme • Remains in the tonic key Cadence theme • Remains in the tonic key

There are three optional elements a composer *could* have chosen to use in sonata form.

1. **Coda**: Composers could add a coda at the end of the recapitulation. The word "coda" means "tail." The purpose of a coda was to extend the final cadence theme and make the final cadence feel extremely conclusive. Often the coda repeated the tonic many times to really pound it into the listener that the piece had arrived "home."
2. Repeat of the exposition: Composers could choose to insert a repeat sign at the end of the exposition. A repeat sign indicated that the performers should repeat the entire exposition, note for note. Sometimes this could be a bit jarring because the piece jumped from the new key (at the end of the exposition) to the tonic key (at the beginning).
3. Slow introduction: Composers could choose to have a slow introduction before the exposition.

Genres that used sonata form:

Any genre could use sonata form. Opera overtures, orchestral music, chamber music—all regularly featured sonata form. Sonata form was so popular, composers could use it for any movement—in any genre—they wanted. It was most commonly used in the first movement.

FURTHER INVESTIGATION: Listen to practically any first movement of any genre in the Classical Era and try to follow along with sonata form.

SUGGESTED LISTENING:

- Mozart's *Don Giovanni, Overture.* Note: This features a slow intro.
- Mozart's *Eine kleine Nachtmusik, 1st movement.* Well known and relatively easy to follow.
- Mozart's *Piano Sonata #18 in D, K 576, "Hunt," 1st movement.* Not only is there a strong cadence at the end of the cadence theme, but there's also a cadence at the end of the bridge, so don't let that fool you.
- Mozart's *Piano Sonata #5 in G, K 283, 1st movement.* There is a fairly solid cadence at the end of the 1st theme, but it is followed by a fairly obvious bridge, a very pretty 2nd theme, and a long cadence theme.

Form: Variation

Variation form was a form that began with a theme (or main melody) that was followed by numerous variations on the theme. This could be diagrammed as:

A	A'	A"	A'"	A""	A"""	A""""	A"""""
(Theme)	(Var. 1)	(Var. 2)	(Var. 3)	(Var. 4)	(Var. 5)	(Var. 6)	(Var. 7)

There are many ways to create variations of a theme. The melody can be ornamented, paraphrased, assigned new rhythms, and changed from major to minor; the harmony can be varied as well. The possibilities were endless and composers could write as many variations as they wanted (or as would keep the audience's attention).

Each section within variation form can be diagrammed more specifically as well. This chart shows the most common ways composers organized themes and variations. Note: the vertical lines with the two dots is a "repeat sign"—anything between the dots is repeated once.

	A	A'	A"
Possibility #1	|:a:||:b:|	|:a':||:b':|	|:a":||:b":|
Possibility #2	|:a:||:ba:|	|:a':||:b'a':|	|:a":||:b"a":|
Possibility #3	|:a:||:ba':|	|:a":||:b'a'":|	|:a"":||:b"a"":|

Notice in Possibility #3 that the first little "a" is changed slightly in the second part of the theme, which is why it has a prime. Composers might choose to use one of the above layouts for the theme and then one of the other layouts for the first variation and then a completely different one for the second variation; composers could also fragment any of the above options or leave out repeats, like so:

A	A'	A"	A'"	A""	A"'"
|:a:||:ba:|	a'b'a'	|:a":||:b"a":|	a'"b'"	|:a"":|	|:a""":||:b"'"a""":|

<u>Genres that used variation form:</u>

- Any genre in this time period can potentially use variation form.
- Used most frequently in:
  - Symphony
  - Sonata
  - Chamber music
  - Solo piano music

FURTHER INVESTIGATION:

1. Listen to variations from the Classical Era. Pay close attention to the theme to determine which diagram to use to follow along. See if each variation follows the same diagram or alters it slightly (or hugely).
2. Listen to variations with a score in front of you to follow along. (Being able to see the repeat signs printed in the score will help.)
3. Listen to variations without a score and count how many variations you hear.

SUGGESTED LISTENING:

- Mozart's *12 Variations in C Major, on "Ah, vous dirai-je maman," K. 265*
- Haydn's *Symphony No. 31 in D major, Hob1:31, "Horn Signal" (fourth movement)*
- Haydn's *Symphony No. 94 in G major, Hob.I:94, "The Surprise" (second movement)*

Form: Minuet

Minuet form evolved from a Baroque Era dance called the "minuet." The Baroque dance minuet was in triple meter and had a middle section of contrasting music called a "trio" because it was played by three instruments. The basic structure of minuet form—also in triple meter—in the Classical Era was

A   B   A

Minuet Trio Minuet

Note: The trio section in the Classical Era was not limited to three performers—it generally featured the same number of performers as in the minuet sections.

Not surprisingly, the large letters in the above diagram could also be subdivided, like so:

	A	B	A
Possibility #1	|: a :| |: ba :|	|: c :| |: dc :|	aba

Composers could also use primes within the basic structure wherever they deemed appropriate. Here are a few of the possibilities:

	A	B	A
Possibility #2	|: a :| |: ba' :|	|: c :| |: dc' :|	aba'
Possibility #3	|: a :| |: ba' :|	|: c :| |: dc :|	aba'
Possibility #4	|: a :| |: ba :|	|: c :| |: dc' :|	aba

It was also quite common for the trio section to be a different tempo than the minuet sections. This was one of the easiest forms to follow in all of music history. Each phrase was relatively short, and all the repetition helped orient the listener.

Genres that used minuet form:

- Any instrumental genre in the Classical Era could use minuet form.
- Used most frequently in:
  - Symphony
  - String quartet
  - Wind quintet

FURTHER INVESTIGATION:

1. Listen to Classical Era pieces in minuet form (found most frequently in the third movement of practically any Classical Era symphony or string quartet). Use the diagram above to follow along.
2. Look at instrumental scores of pieces in minuet form. Notice how repeat signs are used in the printed music, as well as the term *da capo* or its abbreviation "D.C."

SUGGESTED LISTENING:

- Johann Baptist Vanhal's *Symphony in G minor, Bryan Gm2 (third movement)*
- Franz Danzi's *Wind Quintet in B flat major, Op. 56, No. 1 (third movement)*
- Mozart's *Serenade No. 13 in G major, K. 525, "Eine kleine Nachtmusik" (third movement)*

Form: Scherzo

Various composers began replacing minuet form with **scherzo** near the end of the Classical Era, but Beethoven was the most influential in this change. It is certainly possible to find a minuet in one of Beethoven's multi-movement instrumental works, but they are rare. Scherzo followed the same pattern as the minuet (see previous entry). The same diagram could be followed, but there were some differences:

- The scherzo was much faster than the minuet which meant that the triple meter feel was sped up considerably (so that dancing to it would be quite awkward).
- There was more freedom with the structure, so, for instance the 2nd "a" in the first section could be considerably altered or extended (more than would have occurred in minuet form).

Genres that used scherzo:

- Symphony
- String quartet
- Other chamber music

The form became more and more free as time went on. Many composers now write scherzo movements that don't follow the form at all and aren't even in triple meter—but the majority of them are still in a fast tempo.

FURTHER INVESTIGATION: Listen to a number of scherzo movements to see if they follow the form or if they take liberties

SUGGESTED LISTENING:

- Beethoven's *Symphony No. 2 in D major, Op. 36 (third movement)*
- Beethoven's *String Quartet No. 2 in G major, Op. 18, No. 2 (third movement)*
- Beethoven's *Piano Sonata No. 15 in D major, Op. 28, "Pastoral" (third movement)*

Form: Rondo

Rondo form was the form in the Classical Era that allowed the composer the most freedom. Rondo form could be diagrammed in any of the following ways (and many more):

ABABA

ABACA

ABACABA

ABACADABA

And so on and so on …

The one obvious connection between all these possible diagrams is that the A section is repeated numerous times. This form was likely a further development of ritornello form.

The most common diagram for rondo form was

ABACA

As with previous forms in this chapter, each capital letter in the diagram *could* also be sub-divided, like so:

	A	B	A	C	A
Possibility #1	|:a:||:b:|	|:c:||:d:|	|:a:||:b:|	|:e:|:f:|	|:a:||:b:|
Possibility #2	|:a:||:ba:|	|:c:||:dc:|	|:a:||:ba:|	|:e:||:fe:|	|:a:||:ba:|

Also, as with earlier forms in this chapter, composers could choose to use |:a:||:ba:| for the first large A, but then use |:a:||:b:| for the second large A, or vice versa, or they might choose to leave the repeats out for one or more of the larger sections. They may even extend, shorten, or alter (prime) any of the sections at will. It is generally easier to follow along with the larger letters than the subdivisions.

<u>Genres that used rondo form:</u>

- Symphony
- Sonata
- Concerto
- String quartet
- Other chamber music

FURTHER INVESTIGATION:

1. Listen to recordings of pieces in rondo form (often the 2nd movement or 4th movement of a symphony or string quartet). See if you can follow the overall form (usually ABACA) first. Then, see if you can determine if each big letter is divided into smaller letters.
2. Many Classical Era concerti have third movements in rondo form. Listen and notice that in most large sections, when the little letters repeat, the first time features the soloist and the second time features the orchestra.

SUGGESTED LISTENING:

- Beethoven's *Bagatelle in A minor, WoO 59, "Für Elise"* (ABACA)
- Mozart's *Clarinet Concerto in A major, K. 622, third movement* (ABACABA)
- Haydn's *Symphony No. 68 in B flat major, Hob.I:68, fourth movement* (ABACADA+Coda)

Form: Sonata-Rondo

As can be assumed from its name, this was a hybrid of both sonata form and rondo form. This diagram shows traditional sonata form on the left and **sonata-rondo form** on the right.

Sonata Form			**Sonata-Rondo Form**	
A	Exposition	1st theme Bridge 2nd theme Cadence theme	A	1st theme (tonic)
			B	2nd theme (dominant)
			A	1st theme (tonic)
B	Development	Rework earlier material Retransition	C	Development
A	Recapitulation	1st theme Bridge 2nd theme Cadence theme	A	1st theme (tonic)
			B	2nd theme (tonic)
			A	1st theme (tonic)

It is easy to see the relationship between both sonata and rondo form in this hybrid form. It is also easy to see how one might mistake sonata-rondo form for rondo form. To make matters even more confusing, sometimes when composers titled a movement with the word "rondo," it was actually in sonata-rondo form.

Genres that used sonata-rondo form:

- Symphony
- Concerto
- Sonata
- String quartet
- Other chamber music

FURTHER INVESTIGATION: Do an online search for compositions in sonata-rondo form. Listen to them and follow along with the diagram.

SUGGESTED LISTENING:

- Mozart's *Serenade No. 13 in G major, K. 525, "Eine kleine Nachtmusik" (fourth movement)*
- Haydn's *Symphony No. 103 in E flat major, Hob.I:103, "Drumroll" (fourth movement)*
- Haydn's *Symphony No. 100 in G major, Hob.I:100, "Military" (fourth movement)*

Genres of the Classical Era

Symphony

A **symphony** was a multi-movement work for orchestra. The traditional number of movements was four.

The symphony developed out of the orchestral music of the previous time period. Orchestral suites, "sinfonias" (orchestral music within a Baroque opera, oratorio, or cantata), and concerti all had an influence on the development of this genre. The symphony flourished in the Classical Era with the expanding popularity and availability of public concert halls. Because the symphony was fast becoming the orchestral genre of choice, orchestras began to be referred to as "symphony orchestras."

Each movement in the symphony had certain characteristics that remained fairly constant throughout this time period.

The first movement was generally 1) fast, 2) of a serious nature, and 3) in sonata form.

The second movement was generally 1) slow, 2) meant to be beautiful, and 3) in whatever form the composer preferred.

The third movement was generally 1) light in mood, 2) dance-like, and 3) in minuet form.

The fourth movement was generally 1) the fastest of the movements, 2) of a playful nature, and 3) in rondo form.

Occasionally the 2nd and 3rd movements swapped positions. And because sonata form was so popular in this time period, it was often used for both the 1st AND 4th movements.

Performing force: A Classical Era orchestra.

FURTHER INVESTIGATION: Create a playlist featuring nothing but Classical Era symphonies. Set the playlist to "shuffle" and without looking at the titles, try to figure out which movement you are listening to based on the general characteristics of each movement.

SUGGESTED LISTENING:

- Franz Joseph Haydn's *Symphony No. 94 in G major, Hob.I:94, "The Surprise"*
- Wolfgang Amadeus Mozart's *Symphony No. 41 in C major, K. 551, "Jupiter"*
- Ludwig van Beethoven's *Symphony No. 1 in C major, Op. 21*

Exceptions to the definition above: Historically, the word "symphony" has been used in a variety of different ways. The word "symphony" comes from the Greek and means "together sounding." In the Renaissance, it was used for compositions that featured both voices and instruments. In the Baroque Era it was a single movement within a large-scale work. Do not be surprised if you see the word "symphony" or some variant of it used in a different way prior to the Classical Era.

Concerto

The Classical concerto was similar to the Baroque concerto in that it was a composition for a soloist with orchestra. Concerti grossi were not as popular in the Classical Era as they were in the previous era, partly because the focus was on melody, not polyphony.

Each movement in the concerto had certain characteristics that remained fairly constant throughout this time period.

The first movement was generally 1) fast, 2) of a serious nature, and 3) in sonata form. One important note about the first movement of a concerto is that it was not uncommon for the exposition to first be presented by the orchestra alone, and then repeated with the soloist as the main focus (with orchestral support).

The second movement was generally 1) slow, 2) meant to be beautiful, and 3) in whatever form the composer preferred.

The third movement was generally 1) the fastest of the movements, 2) of a playful nature, and 3) in rondo form.

Note that, unlike the symphony, concerti do not use minuet form.

Performing forces: Solo instrument and Classical orchestra.

Technique used in the concerto: Improvised cadenzas by the soloist.

FURTHER INVESTIGATION:

1. Listen to the exposition of a Classical concerto taking note of the first exposition being played by the orchestra and the repeat of the exposition featuring the soloist. Notice how even though the focus is different in each exposition, the thematic material is the same.
2. Listen to examples of concerti from the Baroque and Classical eras and compare the stylistic differences.

SUGGESTED LISTENING:

- Carl Stamitz's *Clarinet Concerto No. 3*
- Wolfgang Amadeus Mozart's *Piano Concerto No. 16*
- Franz Joseph Haydn's *Cello Concerto No. 2 in D major, Hob.VIIb:2*

Sonata

A **sonata** in the Classical Era was a multi-movement solo for piano OR duo for piano and one other orchestral instrument. In duo sonatas, the piano did not act as mere accompaniment, but was an equal partner in the piece; both instruments had featured moments. As in the Baroque Era, the number of movements was flexible, although three movements was the norm.

Forms used in sonatas: Any of the standard forms popular in the Classical Era, namely sonata form, variation form, minuet form, and rondo form. Keep in mind, if the sonata only had three movements, the minuet form was most likely to be excluded.

FURTHER INVESTIGATION:

1. Listen to piano sonatas and take note of how many movements there are and which forms are used in each movement.
2. Listen to some duo sonatas and notice how the focus shifts constantly between the two instruments.

SUGGESTED LISTENING:

- Piano sonata: Wolfgang Amadeus Mozart's *Piano Sonata #5 in G, K 283*
- Piano sonata: Franz Joseph Haydn's *Piano Sonata No. 60 in C major, Hob. XVI:50*
- Duo sonata: Mozart's *Sonata in G for Oboe KV 379*
- Duo sonata: Ludwig van Beethoven's *Horn Sonata in F major, Op. 17*

String Quartet

The **string quartet** was a chamber genre. The vast majority of string quartets were scored for two violins, one viola, and one cello; however, any combination of four string instruments could be called a string quartet. String quartets generally had four movements. This genre came about as a result of a few possible influences:

1. Domestic performers wanted to perform symphonies in their home. So instead of the usual six violins playing the first violin part, a single violinist would play it. Instead of six 2nd violins playing the second violin part, a single violinist would play it, and so on.
2. The trio sonata of the Baroque Era featured two higher instruments and basso continuo (lower instrument plus keyboard). The string quartet may be a result of replacing the continuo players with viola and cello.
3. Some attribute the birth of the string quartet to Haydn, because he standardized the structure and he wrote over 60 of them.

Forms used in the genre of string quartet: The layout of a string quartet was extremely similar to the layout of the Classical symphony. Movement one was generally in sonata form; movement two was in whatever form the composer chose, often variation form; movement three was in minuet form; and movement four was generally in rondo form (and occasionally sonata form or even the hybrid sonata-rondo form).

FURTHER INVESTIGATION:

1. Look up a number of string quartets. Notice the layout of the movements and how they are similar to the layouts of symphonies. Listen to one to see if the assumptions you made about which forms would be used are accurate.
2. Listen to string quartets by different Classical Era composers. See if you hear stylistic differences with each composer.

SUGGESTED LISTENING:

- Wolfgang Amadeus Mozart's *String Quartet No. 19 in C major, K. 465, "Dissonance"*
- Franz Joseph Haydn's *String Quartet No. 30 in E flat major, Op. 33, No. 2, Hob. III:38, "The Joke"*
- Ludwig van Beethoven's *String Quartet No. 3 in D major, Op. 18, No. 3*

Piano Trio

A **piano trio** was a multi-movement chamber work for piano and two other orchestral instruments, usually a violin and a cello. There was no set standard for how many movements were in a piano trio, but the majority of piano trios had three movements. This genre most likely developed as the keyboard part in a Baroque trio sonata became more than merely a continuo performer and began to take on a much more soloistic role.

Forms used in piano trios: Same as in sonatas.

FURTHER INVESTIGATION:

1. Listen to piano trios and take note of how many movements there are and which forms are used in each movement.
2. Listen to piano trios and notice how the focus passes from instrument to instrument.

SUGGESTED LISTENING:

- Mozart's *Piano Trio No. 4 in E major, K. 542*
- Haydn's *Keyboard Trio No. 16 in D major, Hob.XV:16*
- Beethoven's *Piano Trio No. 6 in E flat major, Op. 70, No. 2*

Wind Quintet

A **wind quintet** was a multi-movement chamber work for five wind instruments, usually flute, oboe, clarinet, bassoon, and horn. The standard number of movements in a Classical Era wind quintet was four, following the same pattern as the symphony. The wind quintet was developed in part to showcase the principal (1st chair) players of wind instruments in the Classical orchestra.

SUGGESTED LISTENING:

- Franz Danzi's *Wind Quintet in G minor, Op. 56, No. 2*
- Antoine Reicha's *Wind Quintet No. 9 in D major, Op. 91, No. 3*
- Giuseppe Cambini's *Wind Quintet No. 3 in F major*

Other Chamber Music

There are as many combinations of instruments in the larger genre of chamber music as there are instruments in the orchestra. Because the string quartet was so popular during this time period, almost all chamber music featured string instruments within it. This led to an unusual development in the way genres were titled. For instance, a "flute quartet" in the Classical Era was a multi-movement work for flute and three strings; a "clarinet trio" was for clarinet and two strings; and, as noted above, a "piano trio" was a piano and two strings.

Forms used in other chamber music combinations in the Classical Era: Although there is not a standard number of movements in this vast array of combinations, three or four movements are common.

FURTHER INVESTIGATION: Enter random instruments and the words "chamber music" into an online search to see the variety of combinations. Listen to them.

SUGGESTED LISTENING:

- Mozart's *Serenade for Winds, K. 361*
- Mozart's *Clarinet Quintet in A major, K. 581*
- Carl Friedrich Abel's *Flute Quartet No. 1 in C major*

Opera

The definition of "opera" in the Classical Era was essentially the same as it was in the Baroque Era. For instance, the types of musical numbers in opera were the same: recitative, aria, ensemble, and chorus numbers. The differences/new elements were:

- Recitative was even *more* secco than before. This was also one of the few places in the Classical Era where you would still hear the harpsichord. Recitative in the Classical Era was much more conversational-sounding, and therefore, more characteristic of actual human behavior.

- Ensembles also became much more realistic. In the Baroque Era, ensemble numbers were practically the same thing as an aria, but with two or three singers instead of a soloist. They were fairly static in terms of moving the plot forward. In the Classical Era, on the other hand, ensemble numbers
  - allowed each performer to sing his/her own individual thoughts and feelings at the same time another character was singing about his/her individual thoughts and feelings
  - allowed the emotions of the characters to change as the ensemble progressed
  - moved the plot forward.

<u>Performing forces:</u> More than one singer (with orchestra). In the Classical Era, Mozart pushed boundaries by having a series of scenes in his opera buffa *The Marriage of Figaro* that started as a duo and ended up with eight singers as part of the ensemble.

FURTHER INVESTIGATION: Watch Classical Era operas. Many online sources have complete operas available for viewing.

SUGGESTED LISTENING:

- Mozart's *The Marriage of Figaro*
- Mozart's *Cosi fan Tutte*
- Mozart's *Don Giovanni*

Singspiel

Singspiel was a type of German opera in which spoken dialogue takes the place of the typical recitative numbers. Most *singspiele* (plural) were comic in nature, but there were a few that featured more serious subjects. *Singspiele* still used aria, ensemble, and chorus numbers.

FURTHER INVESTIGATION: Watch Classical Era *singspiele*. Many online sources have complete *singspiele* available for viewing.

SUGGESTED LISTENING:

- Mozart's *The Magic Flute*
- Mozart's *The Abduction from the Seraglio*

Exceptions to the definition above: Earlier in history, the term *singspiel* referred to an array of dramatic presentations including light comic opera and sacred dramatic presentations.

Mass

The Mass continued to be a vital music genre in the Classical Era. The only obvious change from Baroque to Classical was the style of music.

SUGGESTED LISTENING:

- Mozart's *Requiem in D minor, K. 626*
- Haydn's *Mass No. 13 in B flat major, Hob.XXII:13,* "*Creation Mass*"
- Beethoven's *Mass in D major, Op. 123,* "*Missa Solemnis*"

Composers of the Classical Era

The three most celebrated composers of the Classical Era—Mozart, Haydn, and Beethoven—spent much of their careers in Vienna, Austria. They are known collectively as "The Vienna School." There were certainly other composers of note in this time period, but as time moves on, these three continue to overshadow them all.

Ludwig van Beethoven (1770–1827)

<u>Country</u>: Germany
<u>Interesting facts</u>:

- Known for pushing the boundaries of what was acceptable in music form, structure, and tempo.
- Began to go deaf around the age of 30—a condition that made him contemplate suicide, but he felt there was too much music left in him to end his life.
- Music critics generally criticized his music as breaking too many rules. Performers complained that his music was too difficult and too fast. But he maintained that the musicians he could hear in his head were able to do it and therefore, so could the actual musicians.

Best known for:

- Genre: Symphony
- Composition: *Symphony No. 5 in C minor, Op. 67*
- Highly recommended: *Triple Concerto for Violin, Cello and Piano in C major, Op. 56* especially the third movement.

Franz Joseph Haydn (1732–1809)

Country: Austria
Interesting facts:

- Worked for much of his career for the Esterhazy family (Hungarian royalty).
- Wrote a number of compositions with formal titles followed by a nickname, provided either by his friends or by himself. For instance, the "Surprise," "Clock," "Drumroll," and "Farewell" symphonies, and the "Lark," "Joke," and "How Do You Do?" string quartets.
- After his burial, his skull was stolen by a scientist interested in phrenology—the study of the bumps on the head as indication of skill and talent—not to be returned to the Austrian government until the 1950's.

Best known for:

- Genre: Symphony
- Composition: *Symphony No. 94 in G major, Hob.I:94, "The Surprise"*

Highly recommended: *Symphony No. 45 in F sharp minor, Hob.I:45, "Farewell"* especially the first movement.

Wolfgang Amadeus Mozart (1756–1791)

Country: Austria
Interesting facts:

- Child prodigy—along with his talented sister, he performed at courts all over Europe.
- Wrote in both sacred and secular genres including over 40 symphonies, over 40 concerti, and a myriad of chamber music, solo piano music, and a number of highly influential operas.
- Subject of a movie (*Amadeus*) in which fellow composer Antonio Salieri is depicted as a villain partly responsible for Mozart's death. In real life,

Salieri and Mozart were friendly, worked together on a cantata, and Salieri even taught music lessons to Mozart's son.

<u>Best known for:</u>

- Genre: Opera
- Composition: *The Marriage of Figaro*

<u>Highly recommended:</u> *Rondo in A minor, K. 511*

Other Composers

NAME	DATES	COUNTRY	GENRE
Albrechtsberger, Johann G.	1736–1809	Austria	Organ, Church music
Arne, Michael	c. 1740–1786	England	Songs
Bach, Johann C. F.	1732–1795	Germany	Instrumental, Vocal music
Bach, Johann Christian	1735–1782	Germany	Opera, Instrumental music
Billings, William	1746–1800	USA	Church, Patriotic music
Boccherini, Luigi	1743–1805	Italy	Instrumental music
Boieldieu, François-Adrien	1776–1834	France	Opera
Cambini, Giuseppe Maria	1746–c. 1825	Italy	Instrumental music
Cherubini, Luigi	1760–1842	Italy	Opera
Cimarosa, Domenico	1749–1801	Italy	Opera, Keyboard
Clementi, Muzio	1752–1832	England	Keyboard
Cramer, Johann Baptist	1771–1858	Germany	Keyboard
Czerny, Carl	1791–1857	Austria	Keyboard
Danzi, Franz	1763–1826	Germany	Opera, Wind Quintet
Devienne, François	1759–1803	France	Flute music
Diabelli, Antonio	1781–1858	Austria	Vocal music
Dittersdorf, Carl Ditters von	1739–1799	Austria	Vocal, Instrumental
Dussek, Jan Ladislav	1760–1812	Czech Republic	Keyboard, Chamber music
Fasch, Carl F. C.	1736–1800	Germany	Sacred music
Gossec, François-Joseph	1734–1829	Belgium	Sacred and secular
Haydn, Michael	1737–1806	Austria	Sacred
Hook, James	1746–1827	England	Sacred and secular
Hummel, Johann Nepomuk	1778–1837	Austria	Concerto
Kreutzer, Rodolphe	1766–1831	France	Violin music
Krommer, Franz	1759–1831	Czech Republic	Concerto (wind instr.)

(Continued)

Lebrun, Franziska	1756–1791	Germany	Sonata
Neukomm, Sigismund	1778–1858	Austria	Church music
Paisiello, Giovanni	1740–1816	Italy	Opera
Pleyel, Ignaz	1757–1831	Austria	Instrumental music
Reicha, Antonin	1770–1836	Czech Republic	Wind quintet
Salieri, Antonio	1750–1825	Italy	Opera
Soler, Vicente Martin y	1754–1806	Spain	Opera
Sor, Fernando	1778–1839	Spain	Guitar music
Stamitz, Carl	1745–1801	Germany	Instrumental music
Süssmayr, Franz Xaver	1766–1803	Austria	Opera
Wanhal, Johann Baptist	1739–1813	Czech Republic	Instrumental music
Yost, Michèl	1754–1786	France	Concerto

ROMANTIC ERA (1810–1910)

The Romantic Era was a time of great change in music, art, and literature. The forms and multi-movement genres, with their specific rules, were viewed as too restrictive and artificial. Form was not entirely abandoned, but genres with no set form became the norm. The "absolute music" of the past gave way to the "program music" of the Romantic Era. The art, music, and literature of the Romantic Era focused more on human emotions than ever before.

Instruments in the Romantic Era

Woodwind, brass, string, and keyboard instruments continued to be used and perfected during the Romantic Era. The saxophone was invented in this time period. Even though saxophones are made of metal, they have always been considered part of the woodwind family because they were invented by Adolphe Sax, who played both flute and clarinet and borrowed many elements from each of those instruments.

Performance Venues in the Romantic Era

The church, court, opera house, concert hall, and private home continued to be important performance venues in the Romantic Era. With regard to chamber music, it became fashionable to invite performers and composers into your home for a private soirée with a group of invited friends. Many composers in the Romantic Era received a fair amount of their financial support from wealthy people who wanted to be associated with them.

Compositional and Performance Techniques, Forms, and Style Used in the Romantic Era

Forms: Strophic, Modified Strophic, and Through-Composed

These three forms were used in vocal music, particularly in the area of "art" songs.

Strophic form: Strophic form was when the same music was used for multiple verses of a song. For example, most hymns, patriotic songs, and children's songs are strophic—numerous verses, but the same music is used for each verse.

Modified strophic form: Modified strophic form was when the same music was used for MOST of the verses, but some verses were different or were altered to help further enhance the text.

Through-composed: It is actually a misnomer to refer to this as a form, because "through-composed" meant that each verse had different music in an effort to enhance the text. In other words, there wasn't really a structured form. There may have been repetitive motives, but the exact music (per verse) was not repeated.

Genres that used these forms:

- Lieder
- Other "art songs"
- Some operatic arias

FURTHER INVESTIGATION:

1. Listen to lots of lieder *with* the text (and translation) in front of you. Try to determine the form.
2. Listen to a song cycle to determine which lieder within the song cycle are which form.

SUGGESTED LISTENING:

- Strophic form: Franz Schubert's "Ungeduld" from *Die schöne Mullerin*
- Modified strophic form: Schubert's *Gretchen am Spinnrade*
- Through-composed: Schubert's "Halt" from *Die schöne Mullerin*

Performance Technique: Rubato

This performance technique allowed the performer to speed up or slow down the notes of a piece of music to enhance expressiveness. Certain notes could be stretched out and others could be shortened at the will of the performer. **Rubato** was not indicated in the score, with the exception of "tempo rubato" at the very beginning of the piece. Rubato was entirely up to the performer, which made every performance unique.
<u>Genres that used rubato:</u>

- Any Romantic Era genre could use this technique.
- Most frequently used in character pieces and other solo pieces.

FURTHER INVESTIGATION:

1. Listen to three different recordings of the exact same character piece from the Romantic Era. Each recording *should* be quite different because each performer should utilize rubato in his/her own way.
2. If capable, play a character piece on the piano (or find a piano-playing friend to do so) and try to figure out where your own emotions tell you to speed up or slow down.

SUGGESTED LISTENING:

- Frederic Chopin's *Prelude #7 in A major, Op. 28*
- Franz Liszt's "La chapelle de Guillaume Tell" from *Années de pèlerinage I, S.160*
- Edvard Grieg's "Illusion" from *Lyric Pieces, Book 6, Op. 57*

Compositional Technique: Leitmotiv

Leitmotivs were short melodies or even fragments of melodies that represented people, places, objects, emotions, and intents. Leitmotivs were used in the music dramas of Richard Wagner in the Romantic Era. These short motives allowed him to foreshadow events, alert the audience when a particular character was entering, or even what a character was thinking about. It went much deeper than that, however. Wagner wove these leitmotivs together in such intricacies that scholars today are still identifying (and debating) the hundreds of leitmotivs found in Wagner's music dramas.

Genres that used leitmotivs:

- As mentioned, Wagner's music dramas.
- Liszt used them in many of his symphonic poems.
- Other composers of opera used them after Wagner.

SUGGESTED LISTENING:

- Wagner's *Der Ring des Nibelungen*
- Wagner's *Tristan und Isolde*
- Wagner's *Parsifal*

Compositional Technique: Idée Fixe

Similar to the leitmotiv, the **idée fixe** was a melody that represented a character in a story. "Idée fixe" literally means "fixed idea" or obsession. Unlike the short leitmotiv, the idée fixe was a relatively long melody and generally represented one thing within a larger work. It could change throughout a work to represent change within the character it represented. This term was used mainly by French composer Hector Berlioz. In his *Symphonie Fantastique* and *Lélio* (both large-scale symphonies), the idée fixe represented the main character's "beloved." In *Harold in Italy* (another symphony), the idée fixe represented the eponymous character.

FURTHER INVESTIGATION: First, search online for "idée fixe from *Symphonie Fantastique*," and listen to it many times until you can hum it. Then, listen to any part of Hector Berlioz' *Symphonie Fantastique*. Notice how many times it occurs within the symphony.

SUGGESTED LISTENING:

- Berlioz' *Symphonie Fantastique*
- Berlioz' *Lélio*
- Berlioz' *Harold in Italy*

Style: Nationalism

Nationalism was a musical style in which the composer's nationality or homeland was reflected in some way within his/her music. This was done in a number of ways; the most common types of nationalistic music were as follows:

- incorporating national folk tunes/dances/hymns within new compositions
- composing arrangements of pre-existing national tunes
- composing programmatic works that described some element of the composer's nationality or homeland
- composing music intended to arouse patriotic feelings

There were not too many composers who were exclusively nationalistic, so it may be wiser to label individual pieces "nationalistic."

Performing forces: The possibilities were endless.

FURTHER INVESTIGATION:

1. Listen to recordings of Nationalistic music from your own homeland. Do they remind you of your homeland? Do they stir patriotic fervor or nostalgia?
2. Compare a piece of Nationalistic music from your homeland to a similar Nationalistic piece from another country. How are they different or similar?
3. Compose your own arrangement of a tune from your homeland or nationality.

SUGGESTED LISTENING:

- Czech Republic
  - Dvořák's *Slavonic Dance No. 10 in E minor, Op. 72, No. 2*
  - Smetana's *Má vlast*
- Finland:
  - Sibelius' *The Swan of Tuonela*
- Norway:
  - Grieg's *Peer Gynt Suite No. 1, op. 46*
- Poland:
  - Any of Chopin's "Polonaise" or "Mazurka" piano pieces.
- Russia:
  - Glinka's *Kamarinskaya*
  - Mussorgsky's *Night on the Bare Mountain*
  - Borodin's *Prince Igor* (especially the Polovetsian Dances from Act II)
- Spain:
  - Albéniz's *Iberia*
- United States:
  - MacDowells' *New England Idyls, op. 62*

Genres of the Romantic Era

Lied/Song Cycle

A **lied** was a relatively short song for solo voice and piano based on a German Romantic poem. Lieder (the plural of lied) were chamber music meant to be performed in the comfort of one's living room. The piano often (though not always) acted as a programmatic partner with the voice in helping to tell the story. Sometimes a composer would set each poem in an entire cycle of poetry to music. This collection of lieder was known as a **song cycle**.

Performing forces: Solo voice and piano.

Forms used in lieder (and song cycles):

- Strophic form
- Modified strophic form
- Through-composed form

Note: Lieder are part of a larger genre known as "art songs." The definition of an art song is quite simple: a song for voice and piano. Operatic arias are not considered art songs because they are not intended for voice and piano, they are intended for voice and orchestra.

FURTHER INVESTIGATION: Select some lieder. Read the text without listening to the music. Try to imagine what programmatic elements might be contributed by the piano. Then, listen to the piece to see if you were correct.

SUGGESTED LISTENING:

- Clara Schumann's *Liebst du um Schönheit*
- Robert Schumann's Widmung from *Myrthen, Op. 25*
- Franz Schubert's Der Lindenbaum from *Winterreise, Op. 89, D. 911*

Exceptions to the definition above: Sometimes composers would add an extra instrument to the voice and piano, such as the addition of a clarinet for Schubert's *Der Hirt auf dem Felsen*.

Character Piece

A **character piece** was a relatively short solo piano piece with no set form. These could be considered program music to a degree, although they were not necessarily trying to tell a story; in most cases, they were trying to convey, briefly, a particular emotion, mood, or character.

Titles of character pieces were varied. There were non-programmatic titles, somewhat programmatic titles, and completely programmatic titles. In most cases, character pieces were meant to evoke a feeling, a mood, an image, or a dance.

Non-programmatic titles:

- Bagatelle—literally "a trifle"; a short, light-hearted piece—favored by Smetana and Sibelius.
- Capriccio—literally "whim"; meant to sound as though the performers were making it up as they performed—favored by Brahms.
- Étude—literally "study"; term originated as short pieces intended to help an instrumentalist improve their performing technique—favored by Chopin and Liszt.
- Humoresque—term meant to evoke a good mood; "good humor"—favored by Dvořák.
- Impromptu—meant to evoke improvisation—favored by Schubert.
- Intermezzo—term originated as a short comic opera performed before a more serious opera—favored by Brahms.
- Mazurka—term originated as a Polish dance—favored by Chopin.

- Moments musicaux—literally "musical moments"—favored by Schubert.
- Polonaise—term originated as a Polish dance—favored by Chopin.
- Rhapsody—a through-composed piece often incorporating nationalistic melodies—favored by Liszt.
- Scherzo—term originated with Beethoven, meaning "joke"; in the Romantic Era, meant fast, energetic piece—favored by Chopin.
- Tarantella—term originated as an Italian folk dance—used by many composers.
- Waltz or Valse—term originated as a triple meter dance from Germany—favored by Chopin.

Somewhat programmatic titles:

- Ballade—term originated as a poem about a hero, nature, or mythology—favored by many composers including Chopin and Brahms.
- Lied ohne Worte (Song without Words)—meant to emulate the human voice—favored by Mendelssohn.
- Lyric piece—meant to evoke a short poem—exclusively used by Grieg.
- Nocturne—literally means "of the night"; generally a dream-like piece—favored by Field and Chopin.
- Novelette—term meant to emulate a romantic story—favored (invented) by Robert Schumann.
- Prelude—term originally referred to a piece that occurred before something and was often paired (*Prelude and Fugue*, for example); in the Romantic Era, it was meant to evoke a brief glimpse of an emotion or mood—favored by Chopin.

Programmatic titles:

Because programmatic titles were descriptive, the possibilities of titles for programmatic character pieces were endless. Here are some examples of actual titles (translated) of character pieces by a few composers:

Franz Liszt

- *The Thinker*
- *Marriage of the Virgin*
- *The Fountains of the Villa d'Este*
- *The Mournful Gondola*

Robert Schumann

- *Soaring*
- *Why?*
- *In the Night*
- *Butterflies*

Edvard Grieg

- *The Pig*
- *Wedding Day at Troldhaugen*
- *I Wander Deep in Thought*
- *Have You by Chance Seen My Wife?*

<u>Performing forces:</u> Solo piano.

<u>Performance techniques used in character pieces:</u> Rubato

FURTHER INVESTIGATION: Listen to various types of character pieces. Notice the varieties and the use of rubato.

SUGGESTED LISTENING:

- Chopin's *24 Preludes, Op. 28*
- Brahms' *3 Intermezzos, Op. 117*
- Mendelssohn's *Lieder ohne Worte (Songs without Words), Book 2, Op. 30*

Program Symphony

The genre of the symphony, as it existed in the Classical Era, continued to be popular well into the Romantic Era. Many composers wrote symphonies using the same four-movement structure and same forms as the symphonies of the Classical Era. But another type of symphony evolved in the Romantic Era, known as the **program symphony**. Program symphonies were symphonies that told a story using program music.

FURTHER INVESTIGATION: Select a program symphony to listen to. Obtain the written program so you can read the storyline as you listen.

SUGGESTED LISTENING:

- Mendelssohn's *Symphony No. 3, "Scottish"*
- Berlioz's *Symphonie Fantastique*
- Liszt's *Faust Symphony*

<u>Exceptions to the definition above:</u> In general, program symphonies are fully instrumental, but some composers introduced narration or choral numbers within the symphony to help explain the program further. There are also examples of large-scale orchestral works that appear to be program symphonies but the composer called them something else, like "Symphonic Suite" or "Symphonic Poem."

Concert Overture

A **concert overture** was a single-movement orchestral piece. It was not a traditional overture; for instance, an overture at the start of an opera, oratorio, or suite. Instead, it was one piece among many pieces in a concert. Near the start of the Romantic Era, orchestras had taken to playing the overtures of popular operas or oratorios in concerts. After a while, composers of the Romantic Era decided to write "overtures" that weren't even attached to a larger work. Concert overtures are generally programmatic in nature.

<u>Forms used in concert overtures:</u> Sonata form was used early on, but as time went on, composers quit using forms and concert overtures became less restrictive.

SUGGESTED LISTENING:

- Mendelssohn's *Hebrides Overture "Fingal's Cave"*
- Berlioz's *Rob Roy Overture*
- Tchaikovsky's *1812 Overture*

Symphonic Poem/Tone Poem

A single-movement work for orchestra. This genre evolved from the "concert overture." **Symphonic poems** and **tone poems** rarely followed any set form—they were instead free-flowing in order to tell a story (program music). Some composers wrote multi-movement works (program symphony), or compositions featuring a solo instrument with orchestra (concerto), yet still referred to them as "symphonic poems" or "tone poems." Other composers used different terms to describe them, such as "poematic symphony" or, confusingly, "fantasy-overture."

SUGGESTED LISTENING:

- Smetana's *Má vlast*
- Liszt's *Mazeppa*
- Saint-Saëns' *Danse macabre*
- Franck's *Les Djinns*

Opera

The definition of opera was the same as in previous time periods, but there were a few changes to opera in the Romantic Era. Although there was still the use of recitative, aria, ensemble, and chorus, everything seemed to lean much more toward ensemble. It almost seemed as though Romantic Era operas were one long ensemble number. This was a positive thing when it came to realism. Even though opera by its very definition (a story told entirely through acting and singing) was not exactly realistic, the Romantic composers tried to achieve more realism by attempting to avoid the problems of earlier time periods. The main challenge to realism previously was the fact that every so often the action would come to a standstill while someone sang an aria, or when a chorus occurred. In Romantic operas, even if there was an aria, it generally occurred in a much more realistic way—in most cases, the action didn't stop; the person wasn't necessarily singing an inner monologue. Other characters were more involved in hearing the aria and reacting to it; most arias turned into an ensemble number as other characters began reacting to whatever emotion or concept the soloist was singing about.

FURTHER INVESTIGATION: Listen to or watch a Romantic opera. Note the differences between Romantic opera and Classical opera.

SUGGESTED LISTENING:

- Verdi's *Aida*
- Donizetti's *Lucia di Lammermoor*
- Bellini's *Norma*

Music Drama/*Gesamtkunstwerk*

Music Drama, or ***Gesamtkunstwerk*** (literally "Total Work of Art"), was what German composer Richard Wagner called his own operas. Despite Romantic efforts to make opera more realistic, Wagner felt that most Romantic operas had not achieved a convincing level of realism. His attempts to separate himself from other opera composers led him to coin these new terms for his own operas. The reason he preferred these terms instead of "opera" was that he was striving for a new kind of opera in which the orchestra helped express emotion more directly than mere words can achieve.

He attempted this in a few different ways:

- His groundbreaking use of leitmotivs helped the audience make connections to individual characters more immediately, whether that character was on stage or not.
- The use of what he called "unending melody." The melodies in Wagner's music dramas go on and on, rarely reaching a solid cadence point. This was much more true to real human emotion—not contained in neat, evenly spaced packages, but evolving and developing as each moment passes.
- His own libretti. Wagner was one of the only opera composers in all of music history to act as his own librettist. He felt that in order to create a perfect opera, the same creative force must be in control of both the music and the words. (As a side note, he also influenced the sets, staging, and costuming; he wrote lengthy texts on the philosophy behind his music dramas; and he even designed an opera house that was built to his specifications.)

<u>Performing forces:</u> Romantic orchestra (with a much-expanded brass section) and singers.

FURTHER INVESTIGATION:

1. Search online for "leitmotiv" and "Wagner" as keywords. You will find lots of video explanations/examples of leitmotivs as well as articles and other links that will be helpful.
2. Search keywords "leitmotiv" and your favorite epic movie series (like "Star Wars," or "Lord of the Rings"). You will discover that Wagner's technique of leitmotiv has become incredibly popular, especially in modern film music.

SUGGESTED LISTENING: Wagner's *Der Ring des Nibelungen* (this is a cycle of four operas)

- *Das Rheingold*
- *Die Walküre*
- *Siegfried*
- *Götterdämmerung*

Exceptions to the definition above: Not all of Wagner's operas were referred to as "music drama," nor did they all use leitmotivs. He wrote a lot of operas before he wrote the Ring Cycle.

French Grand Opera

A type of opera in which everything was grand—the length, the cast, and the spectacle.

Length: **French Grand Operas** generally had five acts, as opposed to the normal three (or, at the most, four) found in Italian and German operas. Also, because intermissions occurred between each act, and, presuming that an intermission lasted for fifteen minutes (a conservative length), attending a French Grand Opera was a real commitment.

Cast: Many of these operas featured more than the normal number of leading characters. Most traditional operas had one male and one female lead, maybe two of each, but French Grand Operas could have numerous main characters, a large chorus, and dancers.

Spectacle: Because a lot of French Grand Opera was based on historical events, set designers went to great lengths to re-create historic sites and architecture on stage. Also, the special effects were elaborate, including re-creations of massacres, volcanoes, executions, and ghostly visitations.

French Grand Opera style crossed borders; there are examples of operas in other languages and other countries that fit the characteristics of French Grand Opera.

Unfortunately, because of the cost of producing these operas (set design, large casts) they are performed less frequently than they deserve. Some opera companies produce truncated versions occasionally.

SUGGESTED LISTENING:

- Giacomo Meyerbeer's *Robert le Diable*
- Meyerbeer's *Les Huguenots*
- Meyerbeer's *Le prophète*

Verismo

Verismo (translated as "realism") was a term to describe operas in which humanity was depicted in a realistic way, often focusing on the lower classes, infidelity, and death.

SUGGESTED LISTENING:

- Pietro Mascagni's *Cavalleria rusticana*
- Ruggero Leoncavallo's *Pagliacci*
- Giacomo Puccini's *Il tabarro*

<u>Exceptions to the definition above:</u> There is some disagreement as to what operas qualify as verismo. For instance, George Bizet's *Carmen*, which was all about the lower classes, infidelity, and death, is often excluded from this definition because it is in French.

Paraphrase/Transcription/Arrangement

Paraphrase, **transcription**, and **arrangement** are rewrites of pre-existing compositions for a different instrument or ensemble. This was an opportunity for the composer to show his/her ability to create a new, and sometimes improved, version of a pre-existing piece. If the composer took a particular piece and rewrote it with considerable new material added, this was called a paraphrase of the original tune. If the rewrite was fairly straightforward, changing only the performing forces, this was called a transcription. If a composer changed the style of the piece considerably, sometimes the term "arrangement" was used. Not surprisingly, and somewhat confusingly, many composers used these terms interchangeably.

SUGGESTED LISTENING:

- Liszt's *Grandes études d'après les caprices de Paganini*—originally composed by Paganini for solo violin, transcribed by Liszt for piano.
- Thalberg's *The Art of Singing Applied to the Piano, Op.70, #5: Lacrimosa from Requiem by Mozart*—originally composed by Mozart for orchestra and choir, transcribed by Sigismond Thalberg for piano.
- Reger's *Brandenburg Concerto No. 2 in F major*—originally composed by Bach for orchestra and soloists, transcribed by Max Reger for piano.
- Beethoven's *Symphony No. 2*—originally composed by Beethoven for orchestra, transcribed by Beethoven himself for piano trio (violin, cello, piano).

Ballet

Ballet was a genre in which a story was told (and depicted) wordlessly through music and dance. Although it had its roots in earlier time periods, some of the most-performed ballets of all time originated in the Romantic Era.

SUGGESTED LISTENING:

- Leo Delibes' *Coppélia*
- Tchaikovsky's *Swan Lake*, *Sleeping Beauty*, and *The Nutcracker*
- Adolphe Adam's *Giselle*

Concerto

The genre of Concerto continued to be popular in the Romantic Era. All the major composers of instrumental music wrote numerous concerti. The only real differences from previous time periods were

- Less reliance on form
- Less strictness with the number of movements
- Cadenzas were written out by the composer, as opposed to the improvised cadenzas of previous time periods

FURTHER INVESTIGATION: Listen to a Romantic Era concerto and contrast it with a Classical Era concerto.

SUGGESTED LISTENING:

- Chopin's *Piano Concerto No. 2 in F minor, Op. 21*
- Liszt's *Piano Concerto No. 2 in A major, S125/R456*
- Tchaikovsky's *Violin Concerto in D major, Op. 35*
- Dvořák's *Cello Concerto in B minor, Op. 104, B. 191*

Chamber Music

Chamber Music continued to be a living genre in the Romantic Era. The freedom from form and structure as seen in other genres applied here as well. As mentioned earlier in this chapter, it was fashionable to host chamber music performances in your home. The composer, Franz Liszt, moved solo piano music from the chamber to the concert hall because he wanted larger audiences for his music. Other composers and performers liked the idea and a large variety of chamber music began to be performed in concert halls.

<u>Performing forces:</u> Same as in the Classical Era. A few combinations came to the forefront, particularly the piano quintet (one piano, four string instruments).

SUGGESTED LISTENING:

- Schumann's *Piano Quintet in E flat major, Op. 44*
- Schubert's *Piano Quintet in A major, D. 667, "Trout"*
- Brahms' *Piano Quintet in F minor, Op. 34*

Sonata

In the Romantic Era, the sonata continued to be a popular genre for composers and performers. The definition stayed the same—a multi-movement solo for piano OR duo for piano and one other orchestral instrument. The number of movements was extremely flexible, and the reliance on form was minimized.

SUGGESTED LISTENING:

- Piano sonata: Liszt's *Piano Sonata in B minor, S.178*
- Piano sonata: Chopin's *Piano Sonata No. 2 in B-flat minor, Op. 35*
- Duo sonata: Grieg's *Sonata in A minor for cello and piano, Op. 36*
- Duo sonata: Brahms' *Violin Sonata No. 3 in D minor, Op. 108*

Mass

The biggest change to the genre of the Mass in the Romantic Era was the performance purpose. Many Masses were still written specifically for church services, but a lot of composers wrote Masses to be performed as concert pieces.

SUGGESTED LISTENING:

- Anton Bruckner's *Mass No. 1 in D minor, WAB 26*
- Gioachino Rossini's *Petite messe solennelle*
- Giuseppe Verdi's *Messa da Requiem*

Composers of the Romantic Era

Hector Berlioz (1803–1869)

<u>Country:</u> France
<u>Interesting facts:</u>

- Fell in love with an actress named Harriet Smithson. He became obsessed with her and stalked her for a time. When she rejected him, he tried to kill himself with opium, but instead had a vivid opium-induced dream that he had killed her. He wrote a program symphony—*Symphonie Fantastique*—based on his experience with Harriet and opium.
- Got engaged to another woman, but while he was away on an extended trip, she married someone else. Berlioz planned to get his revenge upon his ex-fiancée armed with two pistols, a bottle of poison, and a maid's uniform.
- A few years later, Harriet Smithson married him.

<u>Best known for:</u>

- Genre: Program symphony
- Composition: *Symphonie Fantastique*

<u>Highly recommended:</u> *Tristia, Op. 18* especially the third movement

Georges Bizet (1838–1875)

<u>Country:</u> France
<u>Interesting facts:</u>

- When he composed the famous *Habanera* for his opera *Carmen*, he thought he had based it on an anonymously composed folk song. After the opera was performed for the first time, Bizet discovered that the melody was actually written by a known composer, Sebastián Iradier, and he added an attribution to the published score.

<u>Best known for:</u>

- Genre: Opera
- Composition: *Carmen*

<u>Highly recommended:</u> *L'Arlesienne Suite No. 2*

Alexander Borodin (1833–1887)

<u>Country:</u> Russia
<u>Interesting facts:</u>

- Full-time chemist, part-time composer.
- A member of "The Five"—sometimes called "The Mighty Five" or "The Mighty Handful"—a group of composers who met with the purpose of creating nationalistic Russian music. The other members were Mily Balakirev, César Cui, Modest Mussorgsky, and Nicolai Rimsky-Korsakov.

<u>Best known for:</u>

- Genre: Opera
- Composition: *Prince Igor*

<u>Highly recommended:</u> *String Quartet No. 1 in A Major*, particularly the third movement.

Johannes Brahms (1833–1897)

<u>Country:</u> Germany
<u>Interesting facts:</u>

- As a young teen, made money by playing piano in bars.
- Preferred to use Classical Era structure and form.
- Used metric displacement to make music in one meter sound as though it were in another meter for relatively short sections within a piece.
- Said he loved only two women in his entire life—his mother and Clara Schumann.

Best known for:

- Genre: Orchestral and Chamber music
- Composition: *Ein Deutsches Requiem*

Highly recommended: *Piano Quintet in F minor, Op. 34*, especially the third movement.

Frédéric Chopin (1810–1849)

Country: Poland
Interesting facts:

- Plagued with a persistent cough throughout his life.
- During a revolution in Poland, his friends encouraged him to move away; they feared he was too weak to survive otherwise. He moved to Paris, but honored his homeland with many nationalistic compositions evoking dances and folk tunes of his native land.
- Had a lengthy affair with Aurora Dudevant (an author with the pen name of George Sand). Their relationship ended after she wrote a novel—*Lucrezia Floriani*—that struck a little too close to home; it was about a woman who unhappily took care of a sickly man.

Best known for:

- Genre: Character pieces
- Composition: *24 Preludes, Op. 28*

Highly recommended: *Piano Concerto No. 1 in E minor, Op. 11*

Edvard Grieg (1843–1907)

Country: Norway
Interesting facts:

- Nationalistic composer who tried to evoke and illustrate Norwegian mythology and folklore in his programmatic music.

Best known for:

- Genre: Program music
- Composition: *Peer Gynt Suite No. 1, Op. 46*

Highly recommended: *Wedding day at Troldhaugen, Op. 65*

Franz Liszt (1811–1886)

Country: Hungary
Interesting facts:

- A virtuoso pianist who toured extensively, Liszt had rabid fans who would gather outside his hotel calling his name. He had many affairs including some scandalous ones with the Countess Marie d'Agoult (she later became an author under the pen name of Daniel Stern) and the Princess Carolyn Sayn-Wittgenstein (also an author).
- In his later years, he settled down and took holy orders and was known as Abbé (a religious title) Liszt.
- Invented the concept of the solo piano recital.

Best known for:

- Genre: Piano works
- Composition: *Hungarian Rhapsody No. 2 in C sharp minor*

Highly recommended: *Der Tanz in der Dorfschenke, S514/R181, "Mephisto Waltz No. 1"*

Gustav Mahler (1800–1911)

Country: Austria
Interesting facts:

- While conductor at the Vienna State Opera House, established new etiquette "rules" for classical music audiences, including silence between movements, a rule that has remained in force to this day.
- Preferred to spend his summers in the countryside or mountains composing music in a small hut with nature surrounding him to inspire him.

Best known for:

- Genre: Symphony
- Composition: *Symphony No. 5 in C sharp minor*

Highly recommended: *Symphony No. 2 in C minor, "Resurrection"*

Felix Mendelssohn (1809–1847)

Country: Germany
Interesting facts:

- Composed a number of programmatic works that evoked images of various countries. Among the most famous of these are *Hebrides Overture "Fingal's Cave"* about the island of Staffa off the west coast of Scotland, and his *Symphony #3 "Scottish,"* and *Symphony #4 "Italian."*
- When he received the news that his sister had died unexpectedly, he collapsed of shock and struck his head. He never recovered and died later that same year.

Best known for:

- Genre: Orchestral program music
- Composition: *A Midsummer Night's Dream, Op. 61*

Highly recommended: *Symphony #3 "Scottish"* especially the third movement.

Franz Schubert (1797–1828)

Country: Austria
Interesting facts:

- His admirers would hold social gatherings in their homes at which the music of Schubert would be performed. These events were called "Schubertiaden" (Schubertiades).

Best known for:

- Genre: The lied. He wrote over 600 lieder.
- Composition: *Piano Quintet in A, "The Trout Quintet," D.667*

Highly recommended: "Der Doppelgänger" from *Schwanengesang, D. 957*

Robert Schumann (1810–1856)

<u>Country:</u> Germany
<u>Interesting facts:</u>

- Was planning on a career as a concert pianist, but, after injuring his pinky fingers irreparably, he turned his efforts toward composition. (He was injured after he invented a spring device to strengthen his pinky fingers in an effort to play with as much power as Franz Liszt, a pianist he admired greatly.)
- Fell in love with his piano teacher's daughter when she was 17. Her father was opposed to the marriage, but said they could marry if they waited until she was 21. They eloped the night before her 21st birthday.
- Had a mental illness (likely bipolar disorder) and committed himself to an asylum for the last two years of his life.

<u>Best known for:</u>

- Genre: Character pieces
- Composition: *Carnaval, Op. 9*

<u>Highly recommended:</u> *Theme and Variations in E flat major*

Clara Schumann (1819–1896)

<u>Country:</u> Germany
<u>Interesting facts:</u>

- Her father wanted her to have a career as a concert pianist—a very unusual parental wish for this time period.
- Renowned as a concert pianist. Toured Europe frequently as a performer.
- Taught piano and had many accomplished pupils.
- Mother of eight.

<u>Best known for:</u>

- Genre: Piano music
- Composition: *Piano Concerto in A minor, Op. 7*

<u>Highly recommended:</u> *Liebst du um Schonheit, Op. 12, No. 4*

Bedřich Smetana (1824–1884)

<u>Country:</u> Czech Republic
<u>Interesting facts:</u>

- Very Nationalistic. Wrote a number of programmatic works inspired by his country. Also wrote a number of operas in Czech, the most famous of these, *The Bartered Bride*, emulated Czech folk music.
- In the final movement of "Má vlast" there is a high-pitched note that represents the sound he heard in his head as his deafness increased throughout the last ten years of his life.

<u>Best known for:</u>

- Genre: Opera
- Composition: *The Bartered Bride*

<u>Highly recommended:</u> "Vltava" from *Má vlast (My Country)*

Pyotr Ilyich Tchaikovsky (1840–1893)

<u>Country:</u> Russia
<u>Interesting facts:</u>

- A wealthy railroad heiress, Nadezhda von Meck, admired Tchaikovsky's compositions and began to provide him a yearly allowance so he wouldn't have to worry about money and could, therefore, concentrate on composing. They had a 13-year letter-writing relationship, but never spoke face to face. They felt it would ruin their relationship if they ever met. Then, with no warning or explanation, she quit writing to him.
- Died of drinking unboiled water during a cholera epidemic. Scholars debate whether he did this to commit suicide or if he was forced to do it to prevent a scandal (involving a previous homosexual relationship with a member of the nobility).

<u>Best known for:</u>

- Genre: Ballet
- Composition: *Nutcracker*

<u>Highly recommended:</u> *Symphony No. 2 in C minor, Op. 17, "Little Russian"*

Giuseppe Verdi (1813–1901)

Country: Italy
Interesting facts:

- After writing operas for many years, he retired in 1870 and enjoyed his wealth and his successful farm. About fifteen years after his "retirement" he wrote two more operas, one comic (*Falstaff*) and one serious (*Otello*). He lived another fifteen years after that.
- When he died, he left money to numerous charities. Perhaps the most impressive charitable act began before he died. He oversaw the building of a large home in Milan that had a chapel, a concert hall, a dining room, a ballet studio, rehearsal halls, and lots of apartments. It was built as a retirement home for musicians, conductors, and dancers who had nowhere else to go. He also left behind a sizable endowed fund to keep the home running for many years. After his death he was buried in a tomb in the courtyard. The home is still in operation to this day.

Best known for:

- Genre: Opera
- Composition: *Aida*

Highly recommended: *Messa da Requiem* especially the "Dies Irae."

Richard Wagner (1813–1883)

Country: Germany
Interesting facts:

- Felt that the perfect opera could not be created through collaboration, but must be created by one brilliant mind. He thus wrote his own libretti and music.
- Was so admired by King Ludwig II of Bavaria that he was given the necessary funds to build his dream opera house in Bayreuth, Germany. The entire Ring Cycle (a tetralogy of music dramas) is performed almost every summer in Bayreuth; over 500,000 people try to obtain tickets, but only 58,000 are available each year. Obtaining tickets is an arduous process involving yearly applications (if you miss applying one year, your name moves to the bottom of the waiting list). The wait to purchase tickets has been known to take up to ten years.

<u>Best known for:</u>

- Genre: Music drama
- Composition: *Der Ring des Nibelungen*

<u>Highly recommended:</u> *Tannhäuser*, particularly the overture.

Other Composers

NAME	DATES	COUNTRY	GENRE
Adam, Adolphe	1803–1856	France	Opera
Albéniz, Isaac	1860–1909	Spain	Piano works
Auber, Daniel-François-Esprit	1782–1871	France	Opera
Balakirev, Mily	1837–1910	Russia	Orchestra, Nationalism
Bellini, Vincenzo	1801–1835	Italy	Opera
Boito, Arrigo	1842–1918	Italy	Opera
Bottesini, Giovanni	1821–1889	Italy	Double-bass music
Bruch, Max	1828–1920	Germany	Choral, Orchestral
Bruckner, Anton	1824–1896	Austria	Symphony
Chabrier, Emmanuel	1841–1894	France	Opera
Chausson, Ernest	1855–1899	France	Violin, Orchestral
Crusell, Bernhard Henrik	1775–1838	Finland	Opera, Clarinet music
Cui, César	1835–1918	Russia	Opera, Nationalism
D'Indy, Vincent	1851–1931	France	Opera, Orchestral
Delibes, Léo	1836–1891	France	Opera
Donizetti, Gaetano	1797–1848	Italy	Opera
Dukas, Paul	1865–1935	France	Opera, Orchestral
Duparc, Henri	1848–1933	France	Art songs
Dvořák, Antonín	1841–1904	Czech Republic	Symphony
Elgar, Edward	1857–1934	England	Orchestral
Erkel, Ferenc	1810–1893	Hungary	Opera
Field, John	1782–1837	Ireland	Character pieces
Franck, César	1822–1890	Belgium	Symphony
Gade, Niels	1817–1890	Denmark	Orchestral
Glazunov, Alexander	1865–1936	Russia	Orchestral
Glinka, Mikhail	1804–1857	Russia	Opera, Orchestral
Gottschalk, Louis Moreau	1829–1869	USA	Piano, Orchestral
Gounod, Charles	1818–1893	France	Vocal, Orchestral
Humperdinck, Engelbert	1854–1921	Germany	Opera

(Continued)

Lalo, Édouard	1823–1892	France	Opera, Orchestral
Leoncavallo, Ruggero	1857–1919	Italy	Verismo opera
MacDowell, Edward	1860–1908	USA	Piano music
Mascagni, Pietro	1863–1945	Italy	Verismo opera
Massenet, Jules	1842–1912	France	Opera
Mendelssohn, Fanny	1805–1847	Germany	Character pieces
Meyerbeer, Giacomo	1791–1864	Germany	French Grand Opera
Moscheles, Ignaz	1794–1870	Czech Republic	Piano music
Mussorgsky, Modest	1839–1881	Russia	Opera, Orchestral
Offenbach, Jacques	1819–1880	Ger./Fr.	Opera
Paganini, Niccolò	1782–1840	Italy	Violin music
Pierné, Gabriel	1863–1937	France	Choral, Orchestral
Ponchielli, Amilcare	1834–1886	Italy	Ballet, Opera
Puccini, Giacomo	1858–1924	Italy	Verismo opera
Reinecke, Carl	1824–1910	Germany	Vocal, Instrumental
Rimsky-Korsakov, Nikolai	1844–1908	Russia	Orchestral
Rossini, Gioacchino	1792–1868	Italy	Opera
Saint-Saëns, Camille	1835–1921	France	Orchestral
Sarasate, Pablo	1844–1908	Spain	Violin music
Sibelius, Jean	1865–1957	Finland	Symphony
Sousa, John Philip	1854–1932	USA	Marches
Spohr, Louis	1784–1859	Germany	Opera
Strauss I, Johann	1804–1849	Austria	Marches
Strauss II, Johann	1825–1899	Austria	Waltzes
Sullivan, Arthur	1842–1900	England	Operetta
Suppé, Franz von	1819–1895	Austria	Operetta
Thomas, Ambroise	1811–1896	France	Opera
Weber, Carl Maria von	1786–1826	Germany	Opera
Widor, Charles-Marie	1844–1937	France	Opera, Instrumental
Wolf, Hugo	1860–1903	Austria	Lieder
Ysaye, Eugène	1858–1931	Belgium	Violin music

TWENTIETH CENTURY (1900-2000)

The twentieth century was a time of great change in the world of classical music. There was more variety in genres, forms, and techniques than ever before. In fact, there were so many diverse types of music, the century should probably be divided into smaller "eras." A major influence in the twentieth century was the fact that every composer was pushing boundaries in an effort to do something completely "new."

Instruments in the Twentieth Century

Woodwind, brass, string, and keyboard instruments continued to be used and perfected during the twentieth century. In addition, there was a huge increase in variety with the advent of electronic instruments and various modifications to standard instruments.

Performance Venues in the Twentieth Century

The opera house, concert hall, and recital hall were the main performance venues in the twentieth century. The church continued to be a venue for sacred music. With the changes in the importance of nobility throughout Europe during the Romantic Era, the concept of court composers died out in the twentieth century. Chamber music, with few exceptions, moved completely out of the chamber and into the concert hall and recital hall.

Styles, and Compositional and Performance Techniques in the Twentieth Century

Style: Impressionism

Impressionism was a style of music in which the composer was trying to convey an impression of something. This was not program music, *per se*, because it did not attempt to tell a story. It existed in the grey area between absolute music and program music—leaning heavily toward program music. There was a dream-like quality to Impressionist music.

"Impressionism" is a term borrowed from the art world. In Impressionist art, painters were not trying to achieve a completely realistic depiction but merely their impression of the subject. Often the focus was more on how light and shadow affect the way one perceives an object rather than on the object itself. In general, Impressionist painters didn't blend their colors on their palette; instead they used swipes or dots of color on the canvas that, when viewed from a certain distance, blended together—in the viewer's eye—to create the color desired by the painter. Impressionist art almost seemed to shimmer; there were no hard edges to any particular object.

Compositional techniques used in Impressionist music:

- Note clusters. Impressionist music features clusters of notes—oftentimes dissonant clusters—that blend into a new "color," just as Impressionist art features clusters of actual colors. In the context of music these clusters are rarely perceived as overly dissonant.

- Unusual scales. Composers often used nontraditional scales to achieve the dream-like quality desired—particularly the **whole-tone scale** (all whole steps, no half steps).
- Static harmony. Instead of the dominant-tonic tension so frequent in Classical Era music, Impressionist music employs chords that do not follow their tendencies. Just as whole-tone scales were used instead of major or minor scales, using chords in non-functioning ways adds to the static quality of Impressionist music.

FURTHER INVESTIGATION:

1. Do an online image search for paintings by Monet, Renoir, Degas, Pissarro, or Seurat to see some different styles of Impressionist Art. Notice the way different artists choose different subjects (for instance, Monet prefers architecture and nature, while Degas prefers ballet dancers). Notice how the colors blend in your eye as opposed to on the canvas.
2. Listen to recordings by the two best-known Impressionist composers—Debussy and Ravel—to see how they are similar or different.

SUGGESTED LISTENING:

- Debussy's *Prelude to the Afternoon of a Faun*
- Debussy's *La mer*
- Ravel's *Jeux d'eau*
- Ravel's *Valses nobles et sentimentales*

Style: Expressionism

Expressionism is a tad tricky to define. In one sense, it was any non-tonal or non-traditional music of the early twentieth century. In the art world, Expressionism referred to non-traditional painting techniques, the use of extreme colors, and harsh or disturbing subject matter and emotions. In music, almost any non-traditional early twentieth-century music from Stravinsky to Schönberg—two composers with radically different sounds—could potentially be referred to as Expressionistic.

FURTHER INVESTIGATION:

1. Do an online image search for paintings by Munch, Kandinsky, Schiele, Kokoschka, Klee, or even Schönberg (the composer—who also painted!) to see some different styles of Expressionistic art. Notice the varyingly unpleasant subjects, color choices, and painting techniques.
2. Listen to recordings of Schönberg, Berg, and Webern to hear different approaches to Expressionistic music.

SUGGESTED LISTENING:

- Berg's *Wozzeck*
- Schönberg's *Pierrot Lunaire*
- Webern's *Four Pieces for Orchestra, op. 10*

Style: Nationalism

As indicated in the previous section, Nationalism is a musical style in which the composer's nationality or homeland is reflected in some way within their music.

SUGGESTED LISTENING:

- United States:
  - Copland's *Appalachian Spring*, *Billy the Kid*, and *Rodeo*
  - Ives' *They Are There*, *A Symphony: New England Holidays*, and *Variations on "America"*
  - Gershwin's *Rhapsody in Blue*, *Porgy and Bess*, and *Three Preludes*
- Sweden:
  - Alfvén's *Midsommarvaka (Swedish Rhapsody #1)*
- United Kingdom:
  - Vaughan Williams' *Five Variants on Dives and Lazarus*, *In the Fen Country*, and *Symphony No. 9*

Compositional Technique: Atonality/Bitonality/Polytonality

Tonality is when a particular piece of music has a tonal center (tonic) or, in other words, when a piece is composed using a certain key (or scale).

Atonality: In the twentieth century, many composers, seeking to do something innovative, began composing music with a complete (or mostly) lack of a tonal center—no tonic. To do this, initially composers would start composing a piece of music and if the music sounded like it was heading too directly to a tonic, or even if the melody itself sounded too tonal (scale-based), they would change the notes to ones that did not sound tonal.

Bitonality: Bitonality is when a composer uses two tonal centers (or keys) at the same time—for instance, the melody might be in A major and the harmony might be in B-flat major. Individually they are perceived as consonant and tonal, but together they are dissonant and bitonal.

Polytonality: Polytonality is when there are two or more tonal centers (or keys) present at the same time. Bitonality is a type of polytonality.

FURTHER INVESTIGATION:

1. Look at the score for *Mikrokosmos* by Béla Bartók and notice how on certain pieces, the right hand is written in one key and the left hand is in a completely different key.
2. Look at the score for the third movement of *Piano Sonata No.2 "Concord, Mass., 1840–60"* by Charles Ives. At the beginning (after one measure) is a section of bitonality.

SUGGESTED LISTENING:

- Béla Bartók's *14 Bagatelles, Op. 6, BB 50*
- Darius Milhaud's "Corcovado" from *Saudades do Brazil*
- Igor Stravinsky's *Rite of Spring*

Compositional Technique: Polyrhythm/Polymeter/ Irregular Meter/Mixed Meter

Polyrhythm refers to two rhythms occurring within the same amount of time, for instance triplets against duples, like this:

Or, polyrhythm can be more complex, like groupings of four against groupings of six, or five against seven or eight, like so:

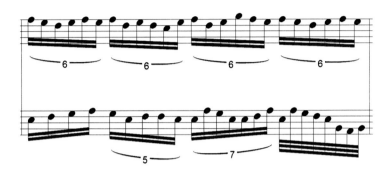

Polymeter, on the other hand, is when multiple meters are occurring at the same time in different lines. In this example, the top line is in 4/4 meter, the second line is in 3/4 meter and the bottom line is in 3/8 meter; even though they're different meters, they fill the same amount of time.

Irregular meters are meters that are not divisible by two or three. For instance, on the following page is an example of 11/16 meter (eleven sixteenth notes per measure):

Other irregular meter possibilities are 5/8, 7/8, and 13/16.

Mixed meter refers to a piece of music in which the meter changes frequently. This keeps the conductor of an orchestra quite busy, not to mention the performers themselves. Here is an example of mixed meter:

This example begins with a measure of four eighth notes, then a measure of two eighth notes, then five, five, and finally three quarter notes. Note that this example also features irregular meters.

FURTHER INVESTIGATION:

1. Obtain a score for any of Igor Stravinsky's ballets. Pick five or six pages at random; you will almost certainly find examples of polyrhythm, irregular meters, or mixed meters.
2. Obtain a score for Paul Hindemith's *Clarinet Sonata*. Notice the use of polymeter.

SUGGESTED LISTENING:

*   Stravinsky's *L'histoire du Soldat*

- Stravinsky's *Petrouchka*
- Hindemith's *Kammermusik No. 1, Op. 24*
- Béla Bartók's *Bluebeard's Castle*

Performance Technique: *Sprechstimme*

Sprechstimme is a technique in which a singer does not sing the pitches indicated, but instead, speaks the pitches. This is indicated in the music by putting a little "x" through the stem of the notes to be spoken on pitch, like this:

In general, as long as singers get close to the pitch indicated, that is good enough. If you listen to multiple recordings of a piece that features *sprechstimme*, each one will sound different because each singer hits the pitches with varying degrees of success.

FURTHER INVESTIGATION: Obtain a score of a piece that uses *sprechstimme*. Note the way it is indicated: either on the note stems or some other way. Listen to multiple recordings of the same piece to hear each singer's interpretation.

SUGGESTED LISTENING:

- Arnold Schönberg's *Moses und Aron*
- Arnold Schönberg's *Pierrot lunaire*
- Alban Berg's *Lulu*

Compositional Technique: Serialism/Twelve-Tone System

Serialism is a compositional technique in which "series" of notes, or other musical elements, are used. It came about largely as a result of Arnold Schönberg's efforts to write atonal music more easily. After composing atonal music for a time, he became frustrated with how much effort it took to avoid a tonic. He came up with a system to ensure that no particular note would be repeated too frequently (i.e., sound like a tonic). He called it the **Twelve-Tone System**. Here's how it works:

- First, create a twelve-tone row. On the piano keyboard, the number of black and white keys between any note and its octave is twelve (A, A#, B, C, C#, D, D#, E, F, F#, G, G#). To create a row, composers would draw the twelve tones out of a figurative hat in random order. Here is what a twelve-tone row could look like:

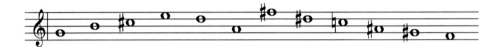

- Once the twelve-tone row has been created, you can begin composing. The rule is that you must use the notes in the row in order. Therefore you *could* choose to use the first three notes as a chord and the next three notes as the melody, then the next three notes as the next chord and the final three notes as the melody, like so:

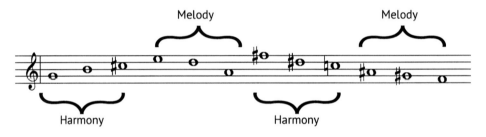

How this grouping would look on the printed music:

In this example, every note is still in the treble clef, but you can change octaves and clefs at will. The only restriction is that you have to use the notes in row order. Then you start over again at the beginning of the row, grouping the notes differently, but *always* in order.

Schönberg knew that one single row could yield only a finite number of options, so he decided that you could turn the row upside down (inversion), backwards (retrograde), and upside down and backwards (retrograde inversion).

Now there are four rows available for use. When you invert a row, the row keeps its shape by maintaining the intervals between each note. Here is an original row followed by an inverted row.

ORIGINAL ROW

INVERSION

When you invert a row, you have the freedom to choose the note on which to start the row—as long as the intervals between notes are maintained, it still has the correct shape. This means that there are twelve possible inversions of the original row. Schönberg decided that the original could also be started on any of the twelve pitches, so there were twelve versions of the original row as well, and the retrograde row and the retrograde inversion row. He came up with a mathematical matrix to be able to quickly figure out his rows:

PRIME ROW →

INVERTED ROW ↓

RETROGRADE INVERTED ROW ↑

0	4	6	9	7	2	11	8	5	3	1	10
8	0	2	5	3	10	7	4	1	11	9	6
6	10	0	3	1	8	5	2	11	9	7	4
3	7	9	0	10	5	2	11	8	6	4	1
5	9	11	2	0	7	4	1	10	8	6	3
10	2	4	7	5	0	9	6	3	1	11	8
1	5	7	10	8	3	0	9	6	4	2	11
4	8	10	1	11	6	3	0	9	7	5	2
7	11	1	4	2	9	6	3	0	10	8	5
9	1	3	6	4	11	8	5	2	0	10	7
11	3	5	8	6	1	10	7	4	2	0	9
2	6	8	11	9	4	1	10	7	5	3	0

← RETROGRADE ROW

With a **twelve-tone matrix**, you have 48 possible rows to use in the creation of a piece of serialist music. If composing a work for orchestra, one of the inverted rows could be used in the violin melody, a retrograde inverted row could be used in the woodwinds, a prime row could be used for the brass, and a retrograde row could be used for the low strings. The possibilities are endless. The creativity of the composer comes into play as he/she decides which rows to use at what time.

Admirers of Schönberg took serialism much further by applying serialist rows to other musical elements. They would create rows of dynamics, rows of note durations, and rows of tempo markings.

FURTHER INVESTIGATION:

1. Create your own twelve-tone row and compose a short piece using only that row over and over.
2. Create retrograde, inverted, and retrograde inverted rows from your original row and compose a short piece using all four rows.
3. Search online for "twelve-tone matrix generator" and create your own matrix.

SUGGESTED LISTENING:

- Alban Berg's *Violin Concerto*
- Arnold Schönberg's *Wind Quintet, Op. 26*
- Anton Webern's *Cantata No. 1, Op. 29*
- Igor Stravinsky's *Agon* (some parts of this work are not twelve-tone and other parts are)

Compositional Technique: Indeterminacy/Aleatory Music

Indeterminacy is a technique used in compositions in which part of the performance is not pre-determined by the composer—certain elements are left up to the whims of the performers. This kind of music is also called **aleatory music** (from the Latin word for "gambling") and **chance music**.

Some examples of indeterminacy:

- A piece in which there is a measure with a number of notes with instructions for the player to play those notes in whatever order or speed they choose to until the conductor indicates it is time to move on.

- A piece in which the performers are instructed to make up their own dynamics throughout the entire piece.
- A composer provides a strange drawing with random lines, squiggles, and shapes and gives no instructions to the performer(s) except that it is indeed music and must be performed.

FURTHER INVESTIGATION:

1. Obtain scores of music featuring indeterminacy and note the endless possibilities in those sections.
2. Read John Cage's instructions to the performers in his compositions *Imaginary Landscape No. 4* and *Concert for Piano and Orchestra*.
3. Go to johncage.org and follow the link "Database of Works" to read descriptions of them. Many of his compositions contain chance elements. Some of them are entirely indeterminate.

SUGGESTED LISTENING: Technically, any indeterminate piece that has been recorded is no longer indeterminate because there is no longer the element of chance. Despite this fact, there are plenty of recordings of John Cage's works, including his most famous (infamous) indeterminate composition: *4'33"*

Compositional Technique: Prepared Piano

John Cage developed **prepared piano** by experimenting with inserting various objects between the strings of a piano to see how it would affect the sound. Eventually he composed many pieces with lengthy instructions itemizing 1) exactly which objects—nails, plastic washers, screws, nuts, bolts—should be inserted into the piano; 2) which strings should be altered in this manner; and 3) precise measurements as to at which point on the string the object should be placed. After preparing the piano, the performer would play the piece using the normal piano keyboard, but the sounds that would emanate from the piano sounded anything but normal, often replicating the sounds of bells, gongs, metallic thunks, and Eastern percussion instruments. The effects of a prepared piano are as varied as the objects that can be used.

FURTHER INVESTIGATION:

1. At johncage.org, there is a link for "Prepared Piano App." The app is free for smartphones. You, too, can create prepared piano pieces!
2. Do an online search for "prepared piano." Watch videos and listen to recordings.

3. Find scores of prepared piano pieces so you can see the instruction list.

SUGGESTED LISTENING:

- John Cage's *A Book of Music (for two prepared pianos)*
- Cage's *Daughters of the Lonesome Isle*
- Ruedi Hausermann's *Schwank*

Performance Technique: Extended Technique

Extended techniques is a term used to describe anything an instrumentalist does to create sound that is outside the normal sounds of their instrument. Here are some examples and how they are notated in music:

Multiphonics: This is when an instrument that was intended to create only one pitch at a time, through a variety of means, is able to create more than one pitch at a time. This includes all brass and woodwind instruments, as well as the human voice.

Instruments as percussion: Any non-percussion instrument (including vocalists) can be struck in many different ways to create different sounds. This can include striking the body of a string instrument; slapping a cupped hand against the opening of a brass instrument mouthpiece, creating a popping noise; and clicking the keys or valves of wind instruments.

Prepared instruments: Similar to prepared piano—inserting objects into the instruments so they react differently than normal. Examples of this include inserting objects into the strings of the violin, viola, cello, bass, guitar, or harp; and various unusual mutes for woodwind and brass instruments.

Flutter-tongue: This technique consists of fluttering the tongue, like rolling an "r" sound, while blowing on a wind instrument. Other methods to achieve a similar effect are making the gargling noise in the back of the throat while blowing, or even humming or singing while blowing.

Pitch-bends and smears: A pitch bend is when an instrumentalist plays a pitch and then, through various techniques, is able to "bend" the pitch downward. Smears are when performers move from one pitch to another in one continuous "smear"; the normal step-wise progression is not heard.

Compositional Technique: Quoting/Borrowing

Quoting and **borrowing** are very similar in that they both use pre-existing music in a new composition. Literally, quoting is when a composer uses a pre-existing piece *note for note* exactly as it was composed. Borrowing, on the other hand, is when a composer uses a pre-existing piece, but arranges it or varies it in some way. It is still recognized as the initial piece, but the composer has reinvented it. (Incidentally, both terms are often used interchangeably.)

SUGGESTED LISTENING:

- Luciano Berio's *Sinfonia, third movement* (quotes the third movement of Mahler's *Symphony No. 2 "Resurrection"*)
- Aaron Copland's *Old American Songs*
- Charles Ives' *Symphony No. 2* (quotes/borrows numerous hymns, patriotic songs, folk songs, and classical music)

Compositional Technique: Electro-Acoustic Music

Twentieth-century composers enjoyed using electric devices to enhance or create music. When electronic means are employed to create music, the term **electro-acoustic** is used. Live performance may or may not be part of an electro-acoustic music performance. There are many types of electro-acoustic music:

Electronically generated music:

- Tape Music—in the mid-twentieth century, electronically generated sounds were captured on magnetic tape.
- Synthesizers—a musical instrument, usually attached to a piano-like keyboard, that creates electronically generated sounds. Synthesizers can imitate naturally created sounds or other instruments.
- Computer Music—tape music was replaced by "computer music" when computers began to be used to create electronically generated sounds.
- Sampling—synthesizers and computers can both "sample," or record, other sounds and reproduce them at any pitch.

Musique concrète: Recorded sounds that are played back as part of a musical performance are referred to as "musique concrète." These sounds can be manipulated, fragmented, sped up, slowed down, or played back exactly as they would normally sound.

When attending an electro-acoustic concert, it may strike the audience as initially odd that some of the pieces that are entirely electronically generated are performed with an empty stage. The audience sits, listens to the electro-acoustic music emanating from a sound system and at the end they applaud the empty stage. Audiences can usually cope better with electro-acoustic concerts that have live performers involved as well.

SUGGESTED LISTENING:

- Paul Dresher's *Concerto for Violin and Electro-Acoustic Band*
- Paul Lansky's *The Lesson*
- Charles Wuorinen's *Time's Encomium*

Genres of the Twentieth Century

Chamber Music

Chamber music continued to be a living genre in the twentieth century. The freedom from form and structure that occurred in the Romantic Era continued to affect chamber music in this time period. Also, new instruments and new combinations of traditional instruments became accepted in this time period. As mentioned earlier, chamber music had officially moved out of the private chamber and into recital halls and concert halls.

<u>Performing forces:</u> All the chamber genres mentioned from the Baroque up to this point are still valid performing forces. Two notable "new" chamber genres—the brass quintet and the Pierrot ensemble—have their own entries below.

SUGGESTED LISTENING:

- Dmitri Shostakovich's *Piano Trio No. 2 in E minor, Op. 67*
- Béla Bartók's *Contrasts (for violin, clarinet, and piano)*
- Darius Milhaud's *String Quartet No. 7, Op. 87*
- Karlheinz Stockhausen's *Helikopter-Streichquartett*

Brass Quintet

A quintet made up of two trumpets, one horn, one trombone, and one tuba. Originally, the repertoire for **brass quintets** was made largely of arrangements and transcriptions of pieces composed for other ensembles, but now many composers compose original pieces for this chamber ensemble.

SUGGESTED LISTENING:

- Frigyes Hidas' *Training Patterns for Brass Quintet*
- Malcolm Arnold's *Brass Quintet No. 1, Op. 73*
- André Previn's *4 Outings for Brass*

Pierrot Ensemble

A **Pierrot Ensemble** is a chamber music group made up of one flute, one clarinet, one violin, one cello, and one piano. Sometimes a vocalist or a percussionist is added to the group. This chamber ensemble received its name because the core group plus vocalist were used by Arnold Schönberg in his famous chamber song cycle *Pierrot lunaire*. Many professional chamber ensembles who specialize in twentieth-century music use this same ensemble and the idea caught on. The Pierrot Ensemble is a standard group at most universities with an emphasis on contemporary classical compositions.

SUGGESTED LISTENING:

- Arnold Schönberg's *Pierrot lunaire*
- Morton Feldman's *The Viola in My Life 2*
- Peter Maxwell-Davies *Eight Songs for a Mad King* (Pierrot Ensemble plus percussion and baritone voice)

Symphony

The genre of the symphony continued to be popular in the twentieth century, but, of course, was less structured than before, and the size of the orchestra could vary widely depending on the composer.

SUGGESTED LISTENING:

- Heitor Villa-Lobos' *Symphony No. 6, "On the Outline of the Mountains of Brazil"*
- Sergei Prokofiev's *Symphony No. 7 in C sharp minor, Op. 131*

- Alan Hovhaness' *Symphony No. 31, Op. 294*

Opera

The definition of opera in the twentieth century was the same as in previous time periods, but again, the twentieth century was a time for rule-breaking. Anything was possible.

SUGGESTED LISTENING:

- Virgil Thomson's *Four Saints in Three Acts*
- Benjamin Britten's *Peter Grimes*
- Prokofiev's *The Love for Three Oranges*

Ballet

Ballet continued to be a vital genre throughout the twentieth century.

SUGGESTED LISTENING:

- Darius Milhaud's *Le bœuf sur le toit, Op.58*
- Aram Khachaturian's *Gayane*
- Stravinsky's *Pulcinella*

Concerto

The genre of Concerto continued to be popular in the twentieth century.

SUGGESTED LISTENING:

- Henri Tomasi's *Trumpet Concerto*
- Pierre Max Dubois' *Alto Saxophone Concerto*
- Alban Berg's *Violin Concerto*

Mass

Masses were still composed for the church, but also for the concert hall.

SUGGESTED LISTENING:

- Frederick Delius' *A Mass of Life*
- Francis Poulenc's *Mass in G Major*
- Ariel Ramirez's *Misa Criolla*

Composers of the Twentieth Century

Alban Berg (1885–1935)

<u>Country:</u> Austria
<u>Interesting facts:</u>

- Student of Arnold Schönberg. Utilized similar compositional techniques as his teacher, including *sprechstimme* and atonality, but Berg leaned much more toward a Romantic orchestra and sound.
- A lifelong hypochondriac, he died of an infected bug bite.

<u>Best known for:</u>

- Genre: Opera
- Composition: *Wozzeck*

<u>Highly recommended:</u> *Lulu*, especially "Wer ist das" from Act III, scene 2.

Leonard Bernstein (1918–1990)

<u>Country:</u> USA
<u>Interesting facts:</u>

- Became famous as a conductor when he stepped in at the last minute for the ill conductor of the New York Philharmonic for a live radio broadcast. He conducted the entire program from memory.

- Appointed conductor or guest conductor with some of the top orchestras in the world, including the Israel Philharmonic, London Symphony Orchestra, and the Vienna Philharmonic.
- Often incorporated jazz and pop elements into classical compositions.

Aside from *West Side Story* — a musical theatre piece — Bernstein is best known for:

- Genre: Choral music
- Composition: *Chichester Psalms*

Highly recommended: *Mass*

John Cage (1912–1992)

Country: USA
Interesting facts:

- Loved to pose the question "What is music?" He was constantly challenging his listeners to recognize that any sound at all can be considered music. When asked if it bothered him when audience members made noise during an orchestra performance of a symphony by Mozart, he replied that he accepted audience noise as part of the music.
- Was greatly impressed by his experience in an anechoic chamber (an echoless chamber). He could hear his heartbeat and a high-pitched hum. After leaving the chamber, he asked the technician what the high-pitched noise was and the technician said it was Cage's own central nervous system.

Best known for:

- Genre: Aleatory music
- Composition: *4'33"*

Highly recommended: *Bacchanale*

Aaron Copland (1900–1990)

Country: USA
Interesting facts:

- Studied with Nadia Boulanger (a great composition teacher) in Paris. She felt that the music he was writing as a student was just like all the

European composers she worked with. She encouraged Copland to find an American voice in his music. As a result of her guidance, he became the best-known nationalistic American composer of all time.

- After the many successes of his "American" works, he tried many other compositional styles including atonality and serialism.

Best known for:

- Genre: Ballet
- Composition: *Appalachian Spring*

Highly recommended: *Clarinet Concerto*

Claude Debussy (1862–1918)

Country: France
Interesting facts:

- Preferred to be compared to "Symbolist" poets rather than "Impressionist" painters, but the label "Impressionist" has stuck to him through the years.
- Uses lots of tone clusters and eastern scales to create a dream-like, hazy quality to his music.

Best known for:

- Genre: Character pieces
- Composition: *Clair de lune*

Highly recommended: *La mer*

George Gershwin (1898–1937)

Country: USA
Interesting facts:

- His first musical job was working as a performing salesman for a music publisher. Gershwin would sit at a piano, and customers would select sheet music (mostly Broadway show tunes) and bring them to him. He would sing and play the songs so they could decide if they wanted to purchase the music or not. It was while working here that he realized that he could probably write better show tunes than the ones he was demonstrating.

- After writing musical theater for some time, he branched out into the classical realm and wrote "classical" works with a jazz influence including *An American in Paris* and the opera *Porgy and Bess*.

Best known for:

- Genre: Orchestral and Piano music
- Composition: *Rhapsody in Blue*

Highly recommended: *3 Preludes*

Charles Ives (1874–1954)

Country: USA
Interesting facts:

- There were three childhood memories that greatly influenced Ives' music.
  1. As a child, he loved lying in bed at night with the window open so he could hear his father's band rehearsing in the town pavilion. Another band was also rehearsing at a nearby park, so Ives would hear two bands practicing two consonant pieces at the same time, which created a type of dissonant bitonality.
  2. Similarly, he also was fond of parades, particularly the sound of one marching band fading in the distance while another was approaching.
  3. The sound of the less-skilled members of the congregation singing hymns in church, including their uneven rhythms and inaccurate pitches. Also, the sound of unison singing.
- His career was as an insurance salesman, but he always composed as a hobby. At some point he self-published his music and donated it to university music schools and performing arts organizations and it started to be performed.

Best known for:

- Genre: Nationalistic orchestral music; art songs
- Composition: *The Unanswered Question*

Highly recommended: *Memories: Very Pleasant/Rather Sad*

Francis Poulenc (1899–1963)

<u>Country</u>: France
<u>Interesting facts</u>:

- A member of "Les Six" ("The Six"). A music critic, Henri Collet, gave this label to a group of young French composers because he felt they were following a similar musical path as Dadaist composer Erik Satie. The other members of the group were Georges Auric, Louis Durey, Arthur Honegger, Darius Milhaud, and Germaine Tailleferre.

<u>Best known for</u>:

- Genre: Opera; Orchestral; Sonata
- Composition: *Concerto for Two Pianos and Orchestra in D minor*

<u>Highly recommended</u>: *Dialogues des Carmelites, FP 159*, especially the "Salve Regina" from Act III, scene 4.

Sergei Prokofiev (1891–1953)

<u>Country</u>: Russia
<u>Interesting facts</u>:

- His music is notable for its non-traditional melodies featuring huge interval leaps.
- His composition *Peter and the Wolf* is often used by orchestras and chamber groups in concerts for younger children to help them get to know the different instruments of the orchestra, since each character in the story is represented by a different instrument—bird = flute; duck = oboe; cat = clarinet; bassoon = Grandfather; horn = wolf; and string instruments = Peter.

<u>Best known for</u>:

- Genre: Ballet, Opera, Instrumental music
- Composition: *Symphony No. 1, "Classical"*

<u>Highly recommended</u>: *Cinderella* (ballet)

Arnold Schönberg (1874–1951)

<u>Country:</u> Austria
<u>Interesting facts:</u>

- His early compositions are highly Romantic in style.
- Invented the twelve-tone system to more easily compose atonal music.
- After receiving negative reactions from audiences regarding his and his students' music, he created the *Verein für musikalische Privataufführungen* (Society for Private Musical Performances). This was intended to keep people from booing or hissing at performances of new compositions. Among the rules of the society were 1) invited guests only and 2) no applause.

<u>Best known for:</u>

- Style: Serialism
- Composition: *Pierrot lunaire*

<u>Highly recommended:</u> *Gurrelieder*

Igor Stravinsky (1882–1971)

<u>Country:</u> Russia
<u>Interesting facts:</u>

- At the premiere of *The Rite of Spring*, some members of the audience didn't like the music and began to boo and hiss. Other members of the audience liked the music and told the others to be quiet. One thing led to another and it wasn't long before the audience devolved into a full riot. At first this was upsetting to Stravinsky, but after opening night, the remaining performances were sold out and the audiences were very well-behaved because they wanted to see what all the fuss was about.
- When Disney made the animated movie *Fantasia*, they used *The Rite of Spring* for an extended sequence depicting prehistoric life and the demise of the dinosaurs. Stravinsky was quite upset that Disney hadn't depicted the actual story of the ballet, which involved pagan ritual and virgin sacrifice.

Best known for:

- Genre: Ballet
- Composition: Aside from *The Rite of Spring*, *The Firebird* is Stravinsky's best-known ballet.

Highly recommended: *Dumbarton Oaks*

Anton Webern (1883–1945)

Country: Austria
Interesting facts:

- Student of Arnold Schönberg. Greatly admired serialism and even opined that the perfect piece of music would be one single statement of a twelve-tone row. As a result, most of his music is quite short.
- Died when he was shot by an American soldier during the occupation of Vienna following World War II. He had stepped out of his house after curfew to smoke a cigarette.

Best known for:

- Genre: Aphoristic serialism
- Composition: *Three Little Pieces, Op. 11*

Highly recommended: *4 Stücke, Op. 5*

Kurt Weill (1900–1950)

Country: Germany
Interesting facts:

- Made political statements with his music, which caused him some problems with the Nazi party.
- His music, both classical and popular (musical theatre), contain influences of jazz and folk music.
- Many of the arias and songs from his operas and musical theatre works have been recorded by jazz and pop artists all over the world.

Best known for:

- Genre: Play with music (Musical theatre)
- Composition: *Die Dreigroschenoper (The Three-Penny Opera)*

Highly recommended: *Aufstieg und Fall der Stadt Mahagonny (The Rise and Fall of the City of Mahagonny)* especially "Alabama Song" from Act I.

Other Composers

NAME	DATES	COUNTRY	GENRE
Arnold, Malcolm	1921–2006	England	Neoromantic
Auric, Georges	1899–1983	France	Opera, Ballet, Film
Babbitt, Milton	1916–2011	USA	Serialism, Electro-acoustic
Barber, Samuel	1910–1981	USA	Romanticism
Bartók, Béla	1881–1945	Hungary	Neoclassic, Folk-influenced
Beach, Amy	1867–1944	USA	Piano music
Ben-Haim, Paul	1897–1984	Israel	Orchestral, Nationalism
Berio, Luciano	1925–2003	Italy	Avant-garde
Birtwistle, Harrison	b. 1934	England	Avant-garde
Bloch, Ernest	1880–1959	Switzerland/USA	Opera, Orchestral
Boulez, Pierre	b. 1925	France	Aleatory, Serialism
Bozza, Eugène	1905–1991	France	Post-impressionism
Britten, Benjamin	1913–1976	England	Opera
Busoni, Ferruccio	1866–1924	Italy	Romantic
Canteloube, Joseph	1879–1957	France	Song cycle
Caplet, André	1878–1925	France	Orchestral, Chamber
Carter, Elliott	1908–2012	USA	Avant-garde
Chávez, Carlos	1899–1978	Mexico	Nationalism
Cooke, Arnold	1906–2005	England	Vocal, Chamber
Cowell, Henry	1897–1965	USA	Avant-garde
Crumb, George	b. 1929	USA	Avant-garde
Dallapiccola, Luigi	1904–1975	Italy	Serialism
Davidovsky, Mario	b. 1934	Argentina	Avant-garde
Davies, Peter Maxwell	b. 1934	England	Avant-garde
Delius, Frederick	1862–1934	England	Impressionism
Dring, Madeleine	1923–1977	England	Neoromantic, Chamber
Durey, Louis	1888–1979	France	Choral, Nationalism
Duruflé, Maurice	1902–1986	France	Organ music
Dutilleux, Henri	1916–2013	France	Post-impressionism
Enescu, George	1881–1955	Romania	Folk-influenced
Falla, Manuel de	1876–1946	Spain	Impressionism
Farkas, Ferenc	1905–2000	Hungary	Serialism, Folk-influenced
Fauré, Gabriel	1845–1924	France	Romantic
Feldman, Morton	1926–1987	USA	Aleatory
Fine, Irving	1914–1963	USA	Neoclassic, Serial

Finzi, Gerald	1901–1956	England	Song cycle
Floyd, Carlisle	b. 1926	USA	Opera
Françaix, Jean	1912–1997	France	Neoclassic
Gaubert, Philippe	1879–1941	France	Flute music
Ginastera, Alberto	1916–1983	Argentina	Nationalism
Górecki, Henryk	1933–2010	Poland	Spiritual minimalism
Grainger, Percy	1882–1961	Australia	Folk-influenced
Griffes, Charles	1884–1920	USA	Impressionism
Grofé, Ferde	1892–1972	USA	Nationalism
Hidas, Frigyes	1928–2007	Hungary	Band, Chamber
Hindemith, Paul	1895–1963	Germany	Expressionism
Holst, Gustav	1874–1934	England	Romantic
Honegger, Arthur	1892–1955	Switzerland	Opera, Symphony
Hovhaness, Alan	1911–2000	USA	Symphony
Howells, Herbert	1892–1983	England	Sacred music
Husa, Karel	b. 1921	Czech Republic	Band, Orchestra
Ibert, Jacques	1890–1962	France	Neoclassic, Impressionism
Ireland, John	1879–1962	England	Impressionism
Jacob, Gordon	1895–1984	England	Wind instrument music
Janáček, Leoš	1854–1928	Czech Republic	Folk-influenced
Joplin, Scott	c. 1865–1917	USA	Ragtime
Kabalevsky, Dmitry	1904–1987	Russia	Opera, Orchestra
Khachaturian, Aram	1903–1978	Armenia	Ballet
Kodály, Zoltán	1882–1967	Hungary	Folk-influenced
Larsson, Lars-Erik	1908–1986	Sweden	Orchestral, Chamber
Lehár, Franz	1870–1948	Hungary	Operetta
Ligeti, György	1923–2006	Hungary	Avant-garde
Lutoslawski, Witold	1913–1994	Poland	Neo-classicism, Aleatory
Martinů, Bohuslav	1890–1959	Czech Republic	Neoclassic, Folk-influenced
Menotti, Gian Carlo	1911–2007	Italy	Opera
Messiaen, Olivier	1908–1992	France	Post-impressionism
Milhaud, Darius	1892–1974	France	Jazz-influenced, Neoclassic
Orff, Carl	1895–1982	Germany	Cantata
Partch, Harry	1901–1974	USA	Avant-garde
Penderecki, Krzysztof	b. 1933	Poland	Avant-garde
Persichetti, Vincent	1915–1987	USA	Neo-classicism, Band
Previn, André	b. 1929	German	Tonal expressionism
Rachmaninoff, Sergei	1873–1943	Russia	Romantic

(Continued)

Ramírez, Ariel	1921–2010	Argentina	Nationalism
Rautavaara, Einojuhani	b. 1928	Finland	Neo-Romantic
Ravel, Maurice	1875–1937	France	Impressionism
Respighi, Ottorino	1879–1936	Italy	Impressionism
Revueltas, Silvestre	1899–1940	Mexico	Nationalism
Riegger, Wallingford	1885–1961	USA	Serialism
Rodrigo, Joaquín	1901–1999	Spain	Neoclassic
Roussel, Albert	1869–1937	France	Neoclassic
Satie, Erik	1866–1925	France	Avant-garde
Sessions, Roger	1896–1985	USA	Neoclassic, Serialism
Shostakovich, Dmitri	1906–1975	Russia	Neoromantic
Stanford, Charles Villiers	1852–1924	Ireland	Opera, Orchestral
Still, William Grant	1895–1978	USA	Opera, Orchestral
Stockhausen, Karlheinz	1928–2007	Germany	Electro-acoustic, Serialism
Strauss, Richard	1864–1949	Germany	Opera
Tailleferre, Germaine	1892–1983	French	Opera, Ballet, Piano music
Takemitsu, Tōru	1930–1996	Japan	Avant-garde
Thomson, Virgil	1896–1989	USA	Opera
Tomasi, Henri	1901–1971	France	Orchestral, Chamber
Tremblay, Gilles	b. 1932	Canada	Serialism, Electro-acoustic
Turina, Joaquín	1882–1949	Spain	Nationalism
Varèse, Edgard	1883–1965	France	Musique concrète
Vaughan Williams, Ralph	1872–1958	England	Impressionism, Folk
Villa-Lobos, Heitor	1887–1959	Brazil	Neoclassic, folk
Walton, William	1902–1983	England	Neoromantic
Wellesz, Egon	1885–1974	Austria	Opera, Ballet, Orchestral
Xenakis, Iannis	1922–2001	Greece	Mathematical music
Zemlinsky, Alexander	1871–1942	Austria	Romantic

Section 8

CONTEMPORARY ERA (1960-PRESENT)

Most music history books group all of the music from 1900 to the present and call it the "Modern Era," but as each year passes, it becomes obvious that at some point the Modern Era needs to be divided up into more than one time period. In another 100 years or so, there will most likely be a more obvious dividing line. For now, this book will take into consideration the composers who are still living today (or until very recently) as well as the styles of the last fifty years or so and call this time period—from 1960 onward—the Contemporary Era.

Instruments in the Contemporary Era

Instruments from previous time periods continue to be used and perfected today. In addition, new instruments are being invented.

Performance Venues in the Contemporary Era

The venues in the Contemporary Era are the same as in the twentieth century.

Styles, and Compositional and Performance Techniques of the Contemporary Era

M uch of what was discussed in the chapters about the twentieth century applies equally to this time period. Most of the same styles and techniques continue to be used, including

- Impressionism
- Expressionism
- Nationalism
- Atonality/Bitonality/Polytonality
- Polyrhythm/Polymeter/Irregular Meter/Mixed Meter
- Sprechstimme
- Serialism
- Indeterminacy/Aleatory Music
- Prepared Piano
- Extended Techniques
- Quoting/Borrowing
- Electro-Acoustic Music

Style: Minimalism

Minimalism is another style that has its origins in the art world. Minimalist music features short motives, simple melodies, and simple harmonic progressions repeated over and over again. Minimalist music has a somewhat hypnotic effect as a result. In order to avoid a lapse into boredom, most minimalist composers will change a few notes or harmonies every few repetitions or so to keep things interesting.

There are sub-genres of minimalism called "Post-Minimalism" and "Holy" or "Spiritual Minimalism."

FURTHER INVESTIGATION: Obtain a score of a minimalist composition by Terry Riley, Philip Glass, or Steve Reich and look at it to see if you can see the characteristics of minimalism.

SUGGESTED LISTENING:

- Terry Riley's *In C*
- Philip Glass' *String Quartet No. 2, "Company"*
- Steve Reich's *Nagoya Marimbas*
- John Adams' *Shaker Loops*
- Arvo Pärt's *Spiegel im Spiegel*

Compositional Technique: Phasing

Phasing is a technique in which two (or more) simultaneous performances of a melody, rhythm, or recorded sound fragment gradually get out of sync with each other. In other words, one performance is slightly (very slightly) faster than the other so they "phase" out of sync creating an echo effect at first, then as the phase progresses they sound like a rhythmic imitation, and eventually they phase back into sync as the faster melody finally "catches up" with the slower melody.

FURTHER INVESTIGATION: If you have good rhythm and a friend who also has good rhythm, get the score for Steve Reich's *Clapping Music* and try to perform it. It doesn't phase as gently as the suggested listening below, but it is still a good example of phasing.

SUGGESTED LISTENING:

- Matthew Burtner's *St. Thomas Phase*
- Steve Reich's *Piano Phase*
- Reich's *Phase Patterns*

Genres of the Contemporary Era

A gain, much of what was discussed in the chapters about the twentieth century applies equally to this time period. Most of the same genres continue to be popular.

Chamber Music

SUGGESTED LISTENING:

- David Del Tredici's *Grand Trio*
- David Maslanka's *Wind Quintet No. 3*
- Pehr Henrik Nordgren's *String Quartet No. 10, Op. 142*

Pierrot Ensemble

SUGGESTED LISTENING:

- Joan Tower's *Petroushkates*
- Chen Yi's *... as like a raging fire ...*
- Ethan Wickman's *Winter's Burst*

Symphony

SUGGESTED LISTENING:

- John Adams' *Son of Chamber Symphony*
- John Corigliano's *Symphony No. 3, "Circus Maximus"*
- David Maslanka's *Symphony No. 5*

Opera

SUGGESTED LISTENING:

- John Corigliano's *The Ghosts of Versailles*
- Steven Mackey's *Ravenshead*
- Daniel Catán's *Florencia en el Amazonas*

Concerto

SUGGESTED LISTENING:

- Astor Piazzolla's *Bandoneon Concerto*
- Philip Glass' *Concerto for Saxophone Quartet*
- John Harbison's *Viola Concerto*

Mass

SUGGESTED LISTENING:

- Roberto Sierra's *Missa Latina, "Pro Pace"*
- John Rutter's *Mass of the Children*
- David Maslanka's *Mass*

Composers of the Contemporary Era

John Adams (b. 1947)

<u>Country:</u> USA
<u>Interesting facts:</u>

- His operas have been somewhat controversial, particularly *The Death of Klinghoffer*, because of its subject matter involving a true story in which a group of Palestinians took a cruise ship hostage, ending with the death of a Jewish passenger who used a wheelchair. Some felt that the opera was too sympathetic to the Palestinians; others felt it was too sympathetic to the Jews.

<u>Best known for:</u>

- Genre: Opera
- Composition: *Nixon in China*

<u>Highly recommended:</u> *Short Ride in a Fast Machine*

George Crumb (b. 1929)

<u>Country:</u> USA
<u>Interesting facts:</u>

- He likes to use instruments (and the human voice) in unusual ways. In one piece, the vocalist has to sing through a long cardboard tube and has to sing directly into the piano, which causes the strings to resonate in sympathy. In another piece, instrumentalists are asked to hum, whistle, grunt, and play other instruments in addition to their own, including crystal glasses filled with different levels of water to create different pitches.

<u>Best known for:</u>

- Genre: Avant-garde chamber music
- Composition: *Black Angels (for electrified string quartet)*

<u>Highly recommended:</u> *Ancient Voices of Children*

Philip Glass (b. 1937)

<u>Country:</u> USA
<u>Interesting facts:</u>

- With his chamber ensemble—the Philip Glass Ensemble—Glass was a musical guest on *Saturday Night Live* in 1986.
- Wrote the soundtracks for a trilogy of art films consisting entirely of images of day-to-day life, architecture, machinery, and technology. In order, the titles of the films in the trilogy are *Koyaanisqatsi*, *Powaqqatsi*, and *Naqoyqatsi*.
- Has transitioned into film music and has been nominated for the Best Music award three times.

<u>Best known for:</u>

- Style: Minimalism
- Composition: *Einstein on the Beach*

<u>Highly recommended:</u> *String Quartet No. 3, "Mishima"*

David Maslanka (b. 1943)

<u>Country:</u> USA
<u>Interesting facts:</u>

- He spent 20 years as a faculty member at various schools before deter-mining that in order to truly achieve his desires as a composer, he had to believe in himself and not rely on a 9-to-5 job. In 1990, he quit, moved to Montana, and became a freelance composer. He has made a living off composition commissions ever since.
- Has embraced the Wind Ensemble (band) as a composition medium. He likes to write for bands because he feels they are more open to his music than orchestras.
- He believes strongly that composers need to achieve a meditative state at which point the music itself will tell the composer how to proceed.

<u>Best known for:</u>

- Style: Neo-Romantic
- Composition: *A Child's Garden of Dreams*

<u>Highly recommended:</u> *Wind Quintet No. 2*

Arvo Pärt (b. 1935)

<u>Country:</u> Estonia
<u>Interesting facts:</u>

- Labeled as a Holy or Spiritual Minimalist, Pärt's works consist of simple melodies and harmonies that move and evolve at a very slow pace. They have a hypnotic quality to them.
- Before settling on his now distinctive style, he dabbled in serialism, alea-tory works, and a technique he came up with called "collage technique" in which he borrowed fragments of well-known historical compositions and inserted them into the midst of his serialist compositions. (If interested, listen to *Collage sur BACH.*)

<u>Best known for:</u>

- Style: Spiritual Minimalism
- Composition: *Fratres*

<u>Highly recommended:</u> *Te Deum*

Astor Piazzolla (1921–1992)

<u>Country:</u> Argentina
<u>Interesting facts:</u>

- Played the bandoneón, a type of squeeze-box accordion, and popularized its use in classical music.
- As a teen, had the opportunity to go on tour with a famous tango orchestra, but his father refused to let him go. This turned out to be a good thing since the plane that was carrying the group crashed, killing everyone on board.
- Studied composition in Paris with Nadia Boulanger, the same teacher who had encouraged Aaron Copland to try to find a uniquely American sound to include in his music. She encouraged Piazzolla to find an Argentine sound and he chose to infuse his compositions with the tango and the bandoneón.

<u>Best known for:</u>

- Style: Nationalism
- Composition: *Histoire du Tango (History of the Tango)*. This piece is so popular it has been arranged and transcribed for a myriad of instrument combinations.

<u>Highly recommended:</u> *Fuga y misterio*

Steve Reich (b. 1936)

<u>Country:</u> USA
<u>Interesting facts:</u>

- Used musique concrète in a unique way with his string quartet *Different Trains*. He interviewed a number of people who had experienced different kinds of trains (including his former nanny, a train conductor, and Holocaust survivors), then used fragments of their recorded voices to create melodies, replicating the pitch and rhythm of their speaking voices with the string instruments.

<u>Best known for:</u>

- Style: Minimalism

- Composition: *Clapping Music*

Highly recommended: *Different Trains*

Other Composers

NAME	DATES	COUNTRY	GENRE/STYLE
Bolcom, William	b. 1938	USA	Serialism
Catán, Daniel	1949–2011	Mexico	Opera
Corigliano, John	b. 1938	USA	Neo-Romantic, Avant-garde
Del Tredici, David	b. 1937	USA	Avant-garde, Electro-acoustic
Ferneyhough, Brian	b. 1943	England	Avant-garde
Harbison, John	b. 1938	USA	Neo-Romantic, Avant-garde
Heggie, Jake	b. 1961	USA	Opera
Higdon, Jennifer	b. 1962	USA	Neo-Romantic, Orchestral
Nordgren, Pehr Henrik	1944–2008	Finland	Nationalism, Serialism
Riley, Terry	b. 1935	USA	Minimalism
Rutter, John	b. 1945	England	Choral music
Rzewski, Frederic	b. 1938	USA	Avant-garde
Saariaho, Kaija	b. 1952	Finland	Neo-Romantic, Serialism
Schwantner, Joseph	b. 1943	USA	Post-Impressionism, Minimalism
Sierra, Roberto	b. 1953	Puerto Rico	Nationalism
Tavener, John	b. 1944	England	Spiritual Minimalism
Tower, Joan	b. 1938	USA	Avant-garde
Whitacre, Eric	b. 1970	USA	Choral music
Wuorinen, Charles	b. 1938	USA	Serialism
Yi, Chen	b. 1953	China	Nationalism
Young, La Monte	b. 1935	USA	Minimalism
Zwilich, Ellen Taaffe	b. 1939	USA	Neo-Romantic

POPULAR MUSIC

A s mentioned earlier in the book, the term "classical music" refers to all "art music" from the beginning of time to the present day and the term "pop music" refers to popular music of the 20th and 21st centuries.

Some people have a hard time discerning the difference between pop and classical music. This is certainly understandable because there are some grey areas where the two meet and overlap. Here are a few general considerations to keep in mind to help determine the difference between pop music and classical music.

1. <u>Venue:</u> The location of the performance can sometimes help you determine if you are listening to classical music or pop music. For instance, if you go to a public concert hall or an opera house, you are probably going to hear classical music. If you go to a nightclub or arena, pop music is more likely.

2. <u>Product provided:</u> In the pop world, the product provided to the consumer is a very specific recording a particular artist made in a studio for the purpose of selling it. In the classical world, the product is the actual music score—the printed music. It is purchased by classical musicians who then perform that music in live performances (and on recordings).

3. <u>Target audience:</u> The target audience for pop music is mostly young people who have the cash necessary to purchase the latest release by their favorite pop artists. On the other hand, the target audience for classical music consists of people who have developed a love of classical music and want to

enrich their lives by attending live performances and by listening to quality recordings.

4. Type of publicity: If your initial exposure to a particular musical artist was through a viral video, it's probably leaning more toward the "pop" side of things. If, instead, your initial exposure was at a concert, listening to a classical radio station, or attending a music history class, it's much more likely to be classical music.

Compositional and Performance Techniques of Popular Music

Performance Technique: Covers

A **cover** is when one pop artist records/performs another pop artist's song. The best covers are those in which something is changed to highlight the artist's qualities and to make the cover unique from the original.

FURTHER INVESTIGATION:

1. Watch a pop singing show or singing competition on television. Take note of the covers and notice the unique changes made to the original song.
2. Online, search for your favorite pop song to see if there are any covers of it. Compare and contrast the original with the covers.

SUGGESTED LISTENING: There are literally hundreds of covers of songs by the Beatles. Listen to any of them.

Performance Technique: Improvisation

Improvisation has been around since the dawn of music. We've read about it already in the Baroque Era: cadenzas, basso continuo, da capo arias; in the Classical Era: cadenzas; in the Romantic Era: various character pieces that are supposed to sound improvised (even though they are not); and in the twentieth century: chance music.

In popular music, improvisation shows up most frequently in jazz. Jazz musicians have trained their ears to follow the chord progressions played by the rhythm section and can improvise a melody based on the harmonic support. Interestingly, jazz is an area of music that still uses the modes that originated in the Middle Ages.

In "pop" music, singers often improvise elaborate melismas on a single note in a song. As an example, think of almost any performance of the national anthem you've ever heard by a pop star—lots of improvised melismas.

FURTHER INVESTIGATION:

1. Go to a live jazz performance. You'll see that various members of the jazz group will have a section within a piece of music to improvise for a while.
2. Listen to two different recordings of the same jazz standard. Note how the main melody is the same in both recordings, but the solo sections are radically different.

SUGGESTED LISTENING: Live recordings of Benny Goodman, Miles Davis, or Charlie Parker.

Compositional Technique: Syncopation

Syncopation is a rhythm in which accented notes occur on unaccented beats or at unexpected times. It provides interest to a piece of music and is a common feature of rock and roll and jazz music.

Performance Technique: Scat-Singing

Scat-singing is when a singer improvises nonsense syllables instead of singing actual words.

SUGGESTED LISTENING: Search online for videos of Ella Fitzgerald, Louis Armstrong, or Mel Tormé scat-singing.

Compositional Technique: Sampling

Popular music uses the technique of quoting/borrowing in some of the same ways, but the most common use of quoting/borrowing is a technique known as **sampling**. When a pop artist "samples" another artist's music, it is usually in the form of a musique concrète usage. Rap artists, for example, will take a pre-existing pop song and sample a fragment of it and then repeat it over and over again as a bass line or accompaniment, while they rap on top of it.

FURTHER INVESTIGATION: Search online for "pop music samples" or "sampling pop music" and you'll find plenty of examples.

SUGGESTED LISTENING:

- Original: "It's the Hard Knock Life" from *Annie*. Sample: *Hard-Knock Life* by Jay Z.
- Original: *Under Pressure* by Queen/David Bowie. Sample: *Ice, Ice Baby* by Vanilla Ice.
- Original: "The Lonely Goatherd" from *The Sound of Music*. Sample: *Wind It Up* by Gwen Stefani.

Performance Technique: Source Music

Source music is a technique used in film (or other theatrical presentation) in which the characters on screen provide music by singing/whistling/humming, attending a music performance, or turning on the radio or other sound device. In other words, the "source" of the music is on-screen.

FURTHER INVESTIGATION:

1. If you own any soundtracks, look at the listing of pieces/songs on the soundtrack. If there is a pop song listed and you can't recall hearing it, rewatch the movie to find out where it occurs—sometimes pieces of music are used for very short amounts of time. For instance, in some movies a character may be walking down the street and a car drives past with its stereo system blaring. That is source music.
2. Next time you watch a film, take note of any examples of source music.

Compositional Technique: Underscoring

Underscoring is the music in a movie (or other theatrical presentation) that "underscores" the action, or heightens the audience's experience by programmatically describing the visual action through music. This music is heard by the audience, but unheard by the characters on screen. If it were heard by the characters on screen, they would never go into those woods, or down that dark hallway, because the music would warn them not to. Underscoring can greatly affect the success of a movie. The most effective underscoring is relatively unobtrusive. If the viewer's mind is drawn away from the action on screen because of the music, the composer has not done his job well. Many soundtracks with underscoring also have leitmotivs.

FURTHER INVESTIGATION:

1. Search online for "worst soundtracks" and watch one of the films listed to see how horrible the underscoring is. (Keep in mind, this is in regard to instrumental/orchestral soundtracks—not soundtracks that consist entirely of pop music.)
2. Watch your favorite film and take note of how the underscoring affects your emotions.

Genres of Popular Music

Film Music

Film music, otherwise known as the "soundtrack," is a very important and influential popular genre. Film music can change the entire effect of a movie on the audience.

<u>Silent Films:</u> In the beginning days of film technology, films were completely silent. Audiences were so taken by the moving images, they didn't really care that they were sitting in silence. It didn't take too long for film-makers to realize that they could enhance their silent films with music. Initially, theaters would hire a local pianist or organist to improvise music that matched the mood or emotions of what was going on on-screen. But as time went on, certain film-makers hired composers to write orchestral scores for the films. Then, local theaters would hire a local orchestra to play the score while the movie was shown.

<u>Talkies:</u> When sound became a feature of film, initially film-makers felt that there was no need for a soundtrack because the audience could actually hear the actors—who needs music? But it didn't take long for music to return as a vital component of film-making.

FURTHER INVESTIGATION:

1. Watch a silent film, preferably in a theater with live keyboard accompaniment. Notice how the music is an attempt to match the emotions of the characters on screen.

2. Watch the original 1931 Hollywood production of "Dracula." The original had NO music (except for during the opening credits and closing credits). Then, try to find the 1999 re-release of "Dracula" in which composer Philip Glass was commissioned to provide a soundtrack. There is a noticeable difference in how you feel while you watch the film.

Jazz

Jazz music is a style of music that has the following characteristics:

- Prominent use of improvisation
- Syncopation
- A featured soloist or soloists most often supported by a rhythm section (guitar and/or upright bass, keyboard, drum set) at the least, and a "big band" (a row of saxophones, a row of trombones, a row of trumpets, and rhythm section) at the most.

Jazz evolved from a variety of sources:

- African work songs/slave songs
- African-American spirituals/gospel songs
- Post-slavery blues songs
- Rag-time piano music

Among the *many* varieties of jazz are the following:

- **New Orleans jazz**—small group of performers, usually featuring clarinet, trumpet, trombone, and rhythm section.
- **Swing** or "big band"—a large group of performers (as described above), often led by a featured performer on either a typical jazz instrument or voice.
- **Bebop**—started as a reaction against how commercial swing was making jazz. Usually a trumpet or saxophone soloist supported by a small group of musicians (maybe two or three other instruments) and a rhythm section. Improvised solos in bebop tend to be quite fast and virtuosic.
- **Cool jazz**—a small ensemble with a variety of instruments. Cool jazz is relatively subdued, compared to the aggressive bebop style. Cool jazz pieces tend to be long and more "composed."
- **Jazz fusion**—jazz combined with pop or rock elements such as electric guitar and synthesizers.

All styles of jazz continue to flourish today in clubs and performance venues across the globe.

FURTHER INVESTIGATION:

1. Investigate the local nightclubs and bars to determine if any of them feature live jazz. In many cases, venues will specialize in a particular kind of jazz.
2. Listen to examples of each kind of jazz listed above to see if you can hear the differences.

SUGGESTED LISTENING:

- New Orleans jazz: *Indiana* performed by Louis Armstrong
- Swing: *Just Kiss Me* by Harry Connick, Jr.
- Bebop: *Confirmation* by Charlie Parker
- Cool jazz: *Take Five* by Dave Brubeck
- Jazz fusion: *Honky Tonk* by Miles Davis

Musical Theatre

Musical theatre is a story told through song, dance, and spoken dialogue. It is an American genre that owes at least some credit to opera, singspiel, and operetta (a light, comic opera). It also has its roots in vaudeville, a type of entertainment in early twentieth-century America that featured a variety of short performances from dancers, comedians, animal acts, and acrobats—a variety show. Performers in musical theater generally need to be what is called in the business a "triple threat," meaning that they need to be able to sing, dance, ***and*** act. There are many sub-genres within musical theatre, including:

- **Revues**—these shows are mainly a showcase for good songs; there is usually no storyline. Examples:
  - *Ziegfeld Follies of 1936*
  - *Side by Side by Sondheim*
  - *A Grand Night for Singing*
- **Book musicals**—This does not mean musicals based on novels (although it does not exclude them). A book musical is a musical with a clearly outlined narrative. The song and dance numbers grow out of the plot. Examples:
  - *The Sound of Music*
  - *Fiddler on the Roof*
  - *My Fair Lady*

- Operatic musicals—Musicals that do not have spoken dialogue but are entirely sung. Examples:
  - *Les Misérables*
  - *The Phantom of the Opera*
  - *Passion*
- Movie/TV adaptations—one trend for the past fifteen years or so is re-working a movie (whether the movie was musical or not) into a stage production. Examples:
  - *Shrek the Musical*
  - *Spamalot* (based on "Monty Python and the Holy Grail")
  - *Legally Blonde*
- **Jukebox musicals**—storylines constructed using pre-existing rock or pop songs. Examples:
  - *Mamma Mia* (using the music of ABBA)
  - *Rock of Ages* (pop hits of the 80's)
  - *American Idiot* (music of Green Day)

FURTHER INVESTIGATION: Think of the musical theatre shows your high school produced and determine in which category it belongs.

Rock and Roll/Pop

Perhaps this is the broadest category of all. **Rock and roll** is a musical style that developed directly out of the blues. Early rock artists were blues artists who added a more driving rhythm and a heavier drum beat. **Pop** music means "popular" music. Sub-genres within the larger genre of rock and roll/pop include:

Adult contemporary	Glam rock	Rap
Alternative	Grunge	Reggae
Bubblegum pop	Heavy metal	Rockabilly
Christian rock	Hip-hop	Ska
Country-western	Indie rock	Soft rock
Death metal	K-pop	Surf music
Disco	Muzak	Techno
Doo wop	New age	Thrash
Dubstep	Punk rock	Wizard rock
Folk rock	R&B	Worldbeat

FURTHER INVESTIGATION:

1. Find an online music download site. Look at the searchable list of genres. Find five of the sub-genres listed above that you are not overly familiar with and listen to examples of them.
2. Borrow a friend's iPod/mp3 player to see what genres they have downloaded (with his/her permission, please).
3. Branch out of your comfort zone and listen to some styles that you haven't tried before.

Composers of
Popular Music

T hese, of course, are only partial lists of well-known composers of each genre.

Film Music Composers

COMPOSER	DATES	COUNTRY	FILM(S) BEST KNOWN FOR:
Arnold, Malcolm	1921–2006	England	*The Bridge on the River Kwai*
Bernstein, Leonard	1918–1990	USA	*On the Waterfront*
Copland, Aaron	1900–1990	USA	*The Heiress*
Corigliano, John	b. 1938	USA	*The Red Violin*
Elfman, Danny	b. 1953	USA	*Corpse Bride* *Edward Scissorhands* *Frankenweenie* *Nacho Libre* *The Nightmare Before Christmas* *Oz the Great and Powerful* *Pee-Wee's Big Adventure*
Giacchino, Michael	b. 1967	USA	*The Incredibles* *Mission: Impossible—Ghost Protocol* *Ratatouille* *Star Trek (2009)* *Up*

(Continued)

Glass, Philip	b. 1937	USA	*The Hours* *The Illusionist* *The Truman Show*
Horner, James	b. 1953	USA	*The Amazing Spider-Man* *Avatar* *A Beautiful Mind* *Jumanji* *Titanic*
Newman, Thomas	b. 1955	USA	*Finding Nemo* *The Help* *The Shawshank Redemption* *Skyfall* *WALL-E*
Rota, Nino	1911–1979	Italy	*The Godfather*
Rozsa, Miklos	1907–1995	Hungary	*Ben-Hur* *Spellbound*
Shore, Howard	b. 1946	Canada	*The Hobbit* *Hugo* *The Lord of the Rings* *The Silence of the Lambs*
Williams, John	b. 1932	USA	*The Adventures of Tintin* *Close Encounters of the Third Kind* *E. T., the Extra-Terrestrial* *Harry Potter and the Sorcerer's Stone* *Home Alone* *Jaws* *Jurassic Park* *Lincoln* *Raiders of the Lost Ark* *Saving Private Ryan* *Schindler's List* *Star Wars*
Zimmer, Hans	b. 1957	Germany	*The Da Vinci Code* *The Dark Knight Rises* *Inception* *Kung Fu Panda* *The Lion King* *Madagascar* *Man of Steel* *Megamind* *Pirates of the Caribbean* *Sherlock Holmes*

Jazz Composers

COMPOSER	DATES	COUNTRY	GENRE
Armstong, Louis	1901–1971	USA	New Orleans jazz, Swing
Basie, Count	1904–1984	USA	Swing
Beiderbecke, Bix	1903–1931	USA	New Orleans jazz
Blakey, Art	1919–1990	USA	Bebop
Brubeck, Dave	1920–2012	USA	Cool jazz
Coltrane, John	1926–1967	USA	Bebop
Corea, Chick	b. 1941	USA	Jazz fusion
Davis, Miles	1926–1991	USA	Bebop, Jazz fusion
Ellington, Duke	1899–1974	USA	Swing
Fitzgerald, Ella	1917–1996	USA	Scat-singing, Swing
Gillespie, Dizzy	1917–1993	USA	Bebop
Goodman, Benny	1909–1986	USA	Swing
Hancock, Herbie	b. 1940	USA	Bebop, Jazz fusion
Hawkins, Coleman	1904–1969	USA	Swing, Bebop
Holiday, Billie	1915–1959	USA	Vocal jazz
Marsalis, Wynton	b. 1961	USA	Jazz and Classical
Miller, Glenn	1904–1944	USA	Swing
Mingus, Charles	1922–1979	USA	Bebop
Monk, Thelonius	1917–1982	USA	Bebop
Morton, Jelly Roll	1890–1941	USA	New Orleans jazz, Swing
Mulligan, Gerry	1927–1996	USA	Cool jazz
Parker, Charlie	1920–1955	USA	Bebop
Prima, Louis	1910–1978	USA	Swing
Ra, Sun	1914–1993	USA	Jazz fusion
Roach, Max	1924–2007	USA	Bebop
Shaw, Artie	1910–2004	USA	Swing
Tatum, Art	1909–1956	USA	Solo piano
Waller, Fats	1904–1943	USA	Swing

Musical Theatre Composers

COMPOSER	DATES	COUNTRY	SHOWS BEST KNOWN FOR:
Berlin, Irving	1888–1989	Russia	*Annie Get Your Gun*
Bernstein, Leonard	1918–1990	USA	*On the Town* *West Side Story*
Bock, Jerry	1928–2010	USA	*Fiddler on the Roof*
Gershwin, George	1898–1937	USA	*Girl Crazy*
Hamlisch, Marvin	1944–2012	USA	*A Chorus Line*
John, Elton	b. 1947	England	*Aida* *Billy Elliot the Musical*
Kern, Jerome	1885–1945	USA	*Show Boat*
Larson, Jonathan	1960–1996	USA	*Rent*
Loewe, Frederick	1901–1988	Austria	*Brigadoon* *Camelot* *My Fair Lady*
MacDermot, Galt	b. 1928	Canada	*Hair*
Menken, Alan	b. 1949	USA	*Beauty and the Beast* *Little Shop of Horrors* *Newsies*
Porter, Cole	1891–1964	USA	*Anything Goes* *Kiss Me, Kate*
Rodgers, Mary	b. 1931	USA	*Once Upon a Mattress*
Rodgers, Richard	1902–1979	USA	*Carousel* *The King and I* *Oklahoma* *The Sound of Music* *South Pacific*
Schönberg, Claude-Michel	b. 1944	France	*Les Misérables* *Martin Guerre* *Miss Saigon*
Schwartz, Stephen	b. 1948	USA	*Godspell* *Pippin* *Wicked*
Shaiman, Marc	b. 1959	USA	*Hairspray*
Simon, Lucy	b. 1943	USA	*The Secret Garden*
Sondheim, Stephen	b. 1930	USA	*Assassins* *Into the Woods* *Pacific Overtures* *Sunday in the Park with George* *Sweeney Todd: The Demon Barber* *of Fleet Street*
Strouse, Charles	b. 1928	USA	*Annie* *Bye Bye Birdie*

Webber, Andrew Lloyd	b. 1948	England	*Cats* *Evita* *Jesus Christ Superstar* *Joseph and the Amazing* *Technicolor Dreamcoat* *The Phantom of the Opera*
Wildhorn, Frank	b. 1958	USA	*Jekyll & Hyde* *The Scarlet Pimpernel*
Willson, Meredith	1902–1984	USA	*The Music Man* *The Unsinkable Molly Brown*

Index

CPSIA information can be obtained
at www.ICGtesting.com
Printed in the USA
FSOW02n0315150715
8841FS